Richard Hoehler's memoir about his life in the theater and his experiences directing the incarcerated from behind prison walls, is a moving testament, that for those with an open heart, salvation can be found through art. He gives his actors voice to express their pain, regret and rage with the words of playwrights, and describes their journey with unvarnished compassion. —**Griffin Dunne, Author,** *The Friday Afternoon Club*

This extraordinary book, written in compellingly straightforward prose, will cast a spell over you by the second page and not let you go till the last. From each monologue and scene, a kind of poetic masculinity takes hold of the reader's heart, leaving it suffused in love, in sorrow, and finally, in greatness. Enormous praise to Richard Hoehler. His big little book is a mighty piece of work. —**Mercedes Ruehl, Academy Award and Tony winning Actor**

For theater folk such as myself, we who are in search of a redemptive truth which transcends even great theater art, Richard Hoehler's book, *Acting Out: How a Prison Workshop Broke Free*, is a veritable holy grail. —**Tom Oppenheim, Artistic Director, The Stella Adler Center for the Arts**

A captivating tale of rehabilitation through the art of theater, allowing the actors to be free, be seen, be heard, and ultimately redeemed. A powerful message awaits those willing to listen. —**Andrew Kossover, Former President, New York Association of Criminal Defense Lawyers**

[Hoehler] loves acting, and he loves the underdog, and he understands the power of the theater as safe space. He, too, shows up with doubts and flaws and pain, but with a pay-it-forward sense of how one can be rescued by someone who cares enough to see you and be seen by you. —**Edith Meeks, Executive and Artistic Director, HB Studio**

With humor and humanity, *Acting Out*, tells us how theatre inspires imprisoned men to reclaim their lives. Author Richard Hoehler is heroic telling how the theatre can be an agent for social change. —**David Rothenberg, Author, Founder of the Fortune Society**

Richard Hoehler's long-standing, important role in American theater has offered a great deal for playwrights, cast members, and theater audiences. But, in *Acting Out*, he tells us that theater is not simply about script and performance. It's a broad insight about all human lives, and it's those lives that are most meaningful and important. —**Walt Odets, Author of** *Out of the Shadows*

ACTING OUT

How A Prison
Theatre Workshop
Broke Free

Richard Hoehler

APPLAUSE
THEATRE & CINEMA BOOKS

APPLAUSE
THEATRE & CINEMA BOOKS

Bloomsbury Publishing Group, Inc.
4501 Forbes Blvd., Ste. 200
Lanham, MD 20706
ApplauseBooks.com

Distributed by NATIONAL BOOK NETWORK

Library of Congress Cataloging-in-Publication Data

Names: Hoehler, Richard, author.
Title: Acting out : how a prison theatre workshop broke free / Richard Hoehler.
Description: Essex, Connecticut : Applause, [2025]
Identifiers: LCCN 2024030096 (print) | LCCN 2024030097 (ebook) |
    ISBN 9781493085552 (cloth) | ISBN 9781493085569 (ebook)
Subjects: LCSH: Prison theater—United States. | Arts in prisons—United States. | Criminals—
    Rehabilitation—United States.
Classification: LCC HV8861 .H64 2025 (print) | LCC HV8861 (ebook) |
    DDC 365/.668—dc23/eng/20240802
LC record available at https://lccn.loc.gov/2024030096
LC ebook record available at https://lccn.loc.gov/2024030097

♾™ The paper used in this publication meets the minimum requirements of American National Standard for Information Sciences—Permanence of Paper for Printed Library Materials, ANSI/ NISO Z39.48-1992.

For Derek, Chas, and Islam

In the worst troublemakers lies, logically enough, the most creative potential. The trick is knowing that it's there, then having the courage to reach for it.

—Michael Nagler

Contents

CONTENTS

Author's Note

There are incidents described in this book that are unsettling. There are also numerous acts of goodwill. An institution founded to incarcerate and "correct" those who have grievously erred will undoubtedly employ some with a desire to punish, but also those with a firm faith in rehabilitation. I have met and dealt with both. The prison in which I have worked over the years has many programs that are rehabilitative. I commend the institution for affording these invaluable opportunities to the incarcerated, and I applaud the men who have utilized them.

The population of a medium-security prison consists of those who have been convicted of crimes ranging from drug offenses to robbery to assault to homicide. Those crimes are never ascribed to specific individuals here. My focus is not on what the men have done in the past, but what they are doing now. To further protect everyone's anonymity, most names and places have been changed.

Preface

Sister Marlene, my first real teacher, shattered some deeply entrenched stereotypes and clichés about knuckle-rapping, ear-pulling, horror-story-telling nuns. She may have worn the same habit as the others, but hers was merely a costume. The woman who stood up in front of our eighth-grade classroom every day was anything but the recovering Catholic version of sisterhood: she was a mensch. Sister Marlene looked right *at* you, in your eyes, not over your head or at your solar plexus. Her unspoken message: "I am here to help. I am here because I want to be here."

Sister Marlene had been transferred from an orphanage in Africa to our small elementary school in Carteret, New Jersey. She became *our* missionary, showing us the same devotion she had given the "pagan babies" we only knew from blurry brochures urging our pennies into the mission box. Sister Marlene had known those children, worked with them, watched them live and die. She never called them pagan babies, just babies. When she shared their stories, she gave them faces and histories and souls.

The few months Sister Marlene taught our class were the first time I looked forward to going to school. Looked forward to being looked at. I suspect the reason she was sent away so quickly (she was gone by Christmas vacation) were the extremes to which she went to really *teach* us, extremes that bucked the system and that made us love her so much. She said the only true lessons were out in the world, not in the classroom, and so it was out into the world we went constantly, on class trips to museums, concerts, festivals, films, and the theatre.

When we attended a play, she saw how smitten I was. I hailed from a family of truck drivers and postal workers who would be thrilled with the idea of having a teacher in the family and not so thrilled with the whole struggling artist thing. When Sister Marlene asked—rhetorically, it seemed—what I wanted to be when I grew up, I hesitated, my dreams having been shot down and laughed at so many times before. But the nonthreatening way in which she posed the question freed me to answer it. I told I wanted to be an actor, that I wanted to work in the theatre. Her response was a benediction:

"Then that's what you'll do."

Was it really that easy? Could you really be who you wanted to be? Sister Marlene seemed to think so. She said that without a passion for something we are just treading water instead of swimming, diving, making a splash. I imagine that is what she had done in Africa, and years later, when I learned she left the convent I hoped it was so she could get back to *her* passion.

It has been a lifetime since eighth grade, and I am still working in the theatre, acting, writing, directing—trying my damnedest to do the next right thing regardless of the obstacles, challenges, and naysayers that dog me on the way. And when I teach, I look my students in the eyes, as Sister Marlene looked in mine, and I let them know that I am there because I want to be there. Sister Marlene was my teacher for mere months but her belief in me changed the trajectory of my life. Not just by suggesting that I pursue a dream—but by insisting on it.

I have seen careers and lives ruined by family expectations, educational agendas, casual dismissals, and bewildered stares given in the wrong place at the wrong time to the wrong human being. In the various posts in which I work—inner-city schools, Alternative-to-Incarceration programs, jails, and prisons—I bear witness to dreams deferred to a much further, even hellish degree.

Sister Marlene gave me permission to break ranks and do what I loved to do. She also demonstrated the importance of giving that permission to others regardless of what they struggled with, whether negative conditioning or baggage or a criminal record. She taught me that nothing is more important than following your heart.

1

TUF LOVE

There is a miniature castle planted alongside a narrow country road not far from the Orange County line in upstate New York. Between two small turrets, in dark blue ink, a graceless sign discloses the name of the compound that lies a quarter of a mile uphill, a compound I'll call Ferrisburg Correctional Facility.

Veering left off the state highway, I remember someone telling me that Ferrisburg had originally been a sanitorium. I think about the irony of a place that once made people feel better now being used to make them feel worse. I pass through the first of three sets of hurricane fencing leading to the prison and stop at the speed bump next to the guardhouse door. I look around at the prison grounds, 1,100 acres sprawled over a southern slope of the Catskill Mountains. Coiled barbed wire trims the tops of the twenty-foot fence surrounding the entire facility, its glistening and jagged points unregarded by deer grazing in open areas and groundhogs scurrying freely from yard to yard. A faded red barn in the distance houses the retired New York City police horses used by correctional officers to patrol the vast and hilly terrain. A stunning view of lush hills surrounds us. Scores of the wrens and sparrows of ecclesiastical hymns are perched along the double and triple rows of sharp metal lines strung below razor-edged coils. A terrible beauty.

I am here to teach an acting class for Larry, whom I met after a reading of my play *Fathers and Sons* at the Fortune Society Castle in Harlem. Larry saw in my bio that I taught acting classes at a special-needs academy in the South Bronx and an Alternative-to-Incarceration (ATI) program in lower Manhattan and asked if I would be willing to lead a one-off class at a small theatre workshop that he ran at Ferrisburg.

Six years prior, at a conference in Toronto, I attended a seminar on a growing movement to promote rehabilitation over punishment in correctional facilities. The presenter was a petite, resilient woman in recovery who volunteered at prisons by bringing in Narcotics Anonymous meetings. The first time she had walked into a room full of lifers—massively built, deadly silent men covered with tattoos—she was terrified. But something her churchgoing mother said before seeing her off that day had calmed her: "Remember, honey: they're just God's kids."

That dispelled her fears and prejudices about the felons who stood before her and enabled her to begin what would be decades of meaningful work with the incarcerated. I was deeply affected by her talk and the many stories of hope and redemption. She had walked through her fear and was touching lives. I wondered if I might one day do the same. When Larry shook my hand and thanked me for agreeing to teach the class for his group, I sensed the day had come. When I called *my* mother, also a churchgoing woman, to tell her about my new venture, her advice could not have been more different:

"Be careful."

No Weapons, Cell Phones, Cameras, Laptops, Electronic Devices, Alcohol, Tobacco, Drugs, Explosives, Aerosol Cans.... Wired to the front fence are bold-type signs in English and Spanish forewarning visitors what to abandon before entering here. We hand our IDs to the officer and wait while he checks them against his roster and takes down our license plate numbers. He calls ahead to the arsenal, our next stop, and hands back our IDs. On the other side of the fence, the inmates are walking along the central road of the prison on their way to the program area where I will be teaching. A mass of deep green (New York State's designated color for its detainees) slowly rolls down the hill before us, each man clutching a white, netted see-through bag filled with books and snacks and clothing. Sitting in the car watching the steady migration, I imagine this trek being made for decades, centuries, millennia.

After the men pass through the nexus of the four-way access point to the prison grounds, one set of walls slides shut and another set in front of us slowly opens. As we drive inside, I feel a pull in my chest, an old feeling that has emerged at various points in my life when I am moving into unknown territory. The first time I felt it was back in high school when I stepped off a bus from New Jersey and was overwhelmed by the frenzied energy of midtown Manhattan. We were on a class trip to see *The Me Nobody Knows*, a play created from the writings of inner-city kids—a play that changed everything for me.

I was an overly sensitive kid who grew up in a tough, blue-collar New Jersey town, and I identified strongly with the sentiments of the play: being left out, feeling different, longing to be recognized, included, accepted, loved. My home was certainly not where the heart was. My father was a sick and suffering alcoholic who wreaked terror with his words and hands, and my mom was a frustrated writer often hospitalized with what was then called manic depression. I spent much of my childhood dodging my father's belt and trying to allay my mother's unreasonable fears—both unsuccessfully. Most of my energy went into taking care of my six younger siblings while secretly yearning for an escape.

I cried unabashedly at the end of *The Me Nobody Knows*, not from sadness, but because the strength, beauty, and promise born of the refusal to surrender to adversity ultimately triumphed. I walked dizzily back to the Port Authority Bus Terminal, drunk on humanity and art, with a newfound belief that hopeless could transform into hopeful and that *theatre* was the way to do it. In high school I directed my first play with a cast of unruly third graders. In college I did theatre with at-risk teens in church basements and boiler rooms. In New York I directed plays and taught acting classes in some of the poorest neighborhoods in the city, like those from whence *The Me Nobody Knows* had come.

After parking in a designated space in the lower level of the two-tiered parking lot, we leave our cell phones and wallets in the car and empty our pockets of contraband—gum, candy, breath mints, medication, flash drives, receipts, clickable ballpoint pens, paper clips, *anything* metal. We proceed to the arsenal where we will be processed, waiting outside the heavy black steel-barred door until it pops ajar with a sharp, low buzz. Inside, we hand over our driver's licenses and car keys to the correctional officer stationed behind the bulletproof glass window. Our IDs are cable-clipped and hung on a teacup hook on the inside wall along with our keys. The guard slides an album-like guest book through a slot in the plexiglass window. We write our names, purpose of our visit, and time. We are instructed to remove our shoes, belts, jackets, hats, glasses, and watches before we walk forward and back through the metal detector. We slide our jackets and bags of teaching supplies through the slot for inspection. My neon highlighter is confiscated—because, the officer explains, it can be used to illicitly communicate messages to or from prisoners over great distances. After our hands are stamped with invisible ink, we are buzzed through a second steel-barred door.

We walk down a gleaming waxed corridor toward the dispatcher's office. An inmate wearing a green yarn cap as an accessory to his uniform is damp-mopping the floor and politely warns us to take care. Larry tells the dispatcher, an impenetrable CO—correctional officer—sitting behind an elevated desk, where we are headed. The CO barks into his walkie-talkie and instructs us to wait in the count room.

The count room resembles a thin slice of a gymnasium. Red lines are painted on the floor, along which I assume inmates stand several times a day to be tallied. There is a small podium in the center of the room, a pulpit from where I imagine the count is made. Ironically, photographs of equestrian shows and rodeos are posted around a room in which men are counted like cattle. (I later learn that it is actually the correctional officers who assemble here each morning for their day's assignments. A whole other rodeo.)

Ten minutes later a loud squawk announces that our ride has arrived. We are buzzed through a third steel door and head outside. As we walk to the waiting van, I ask Larry how far it is to Building 112, where the workshop will be held. Larry points to a low bungalow maybe 300 yards away. I once led creative writing workshops at a high school on Rikers Island where, even though the building in which I taught was directly across from the processing center, I was required to board a bus that circled the entire island, making stops and pickups along the way until I was dropped at the last designated point—a hundred yards from where we had started off. What would have been a half-minute walk took almost half an hour.

The gruffness of the dispatcher and the recklessness of the van driver chip away at my resolve. I begin second-guessing whether I am cut out for this. I worry how the inmates will respond to the touchy-feely theatre warm-ups and exercises, which are designed to help them get past the very defenses they need in this oppressive environment. How will the correctional officers react when I do Lotte Goslar's screaming exercise? Will they think I'm some kind a nut? Will they shut us down? As the van carries us down a steep hill toward the program area, we whisk past the men in green, now splintering off and filing into several different buildings—barbershop, law library, chapel, classrooms. Some men have dogs on leashes, future drug and bomb sniffers who they train as part of the Puppies Behind Bars program. The dogs could be anywhere, wagging their tails, sniffing their companions' pant legs, occasionally jumping up for a pat, unconditionally loving the convicts who care for them.

The classroom is not what I expect. I anticipated the dingy, gray walls of television prison dramas and instead I walk into a bright, clean room with colored lettering charts, heartening aphorisms, and pictures of inspirational people of color from American history posted about. Attendance is solid: fifteen men sitting or leaning around the periphery. Everyone rises to a lackadaisical attention when we enter. Before Larry introduces me, I walk to the center of the room, place a small red X with spike tape on the floor, and ask everyone to gather in a circle.

It still mystifies me how unafraid, even at ease, I am with hostile teenagers and convicted felons—the same toughs who would have undoubtedly tortured me in gym class back in the day. As a kid my only contact sport was as a baseball player in our high school production of *Damn Yankees*. I never even tried to compete with the jocks and bullies who ran the school (and often absconded with the leading roles in plays). Instead, I started my own theatre troupe so the ragtag band of misfits I ran with could have our moment in the sun. I found the perfect vehicle in *You're a Good Man, Charlie Brown*. My self-cultivated can't-catch-a-break persona coincided perfectly with the sad-sack hero of the show, and the other roles seemed custom-made for my cohorts. My *Charlie Brown* days served me well. Playing a hapless character who is the star of the show helped me enormously as a teacher. I learned how to stay humble while remaining in command, how to mitigate tone and defuse difficult and challenging circumstances.

I start class with a Check-In: everyone around the circle says their name and, in a word or two, how they honestly feel in the moment, a sort of prime directive to start from "where you are." What I hear is standard:

"Curious… A'ight… Ready… Hungry… Tired… Blessed…"

It usually takes a few classes before everyone feels comfortable enough to really put it out there:

"Angry… Sad… Tight… Scared… I hate this fuckin' place."

Over time, as layers peel away and participants access the truth of where they are emotionally, they find themselves on solid ground where admissions can be made without defenses, and where attitudes and feelings can be expressed honestly without snarky comments, platitudes, or unwanted advocacy. When I taught at a PSY-7 school in Harlem for emotionally disturbed and troubled kids, Keisha, who had spent many years in special schools, told me she loved Check-In. She was all over the map at the top of each class: "My name is Keisha and I'm tight." "My name is Keisha and I'm too sad." "My name is Keisha and don't nobody fuck with me today." She said that no one in any school she had ever attended asked her how she felt.

I turn and look at the man to my right, make eye contact, and clap my hands. He then claps back to me as an acceptance of the gesture and then turns and passes it on to the next actor. The goal of this exercise—"Ripple"—is to establish a steady rhythmic wave of movement around the circle, later reversed and augmented with other interstitial gestures. The men take to it hungrily. I watch as they let go of ego drives and give themselves over to the group, how they stop planning and positioning and throw reason to the wind, surrendering to instinct and having a hell of a good time doing it.

Often, when I introduce Ripple to a new group, they think it silly and childish and only give it a go after I tell them I do the same exercise with professional actors. But whenever we mount a production or showcase, the same actors *beg* to do it before the show. Terrified of performing before an audience for the first time, it is the one thing that calms them down by helping them to stop thinking, dispelling their stage fright.

Occasionally a correctional officer walks by the door, stops, and peers through the small plate-glass window, but for the most part we are left on our own. The absence of hands-on prison supervision helps create a neutral and safe space where the men can drop their defenses and delve deeper and deeper into the work.

A man stands on the X in the center of the room. I leave the circle and walk toward him. I stop, look him in the eyes and say, "Hello." He has been instructed not to respond, simply to acknowledge that he has been recognized. He leaves and I take the X. The next man walks in, stops, looks over my head and says: "'Tsup."

I stop the exercise and tell him the line is "Hello." He rolls his eyes to heaven:

"Don't nobody say *hello* in this place."

"That's the line."

"What about *Yo?*"

"The exercise is called 'Hello,' not 'Yo.' When you do a play, you can't change the lines. And look *at* me, not down the block."

He pans around the room at the other men, shrugs his shoulders, and tries again. He walks back in and really looks at me this time:

"Hello."

I nod and leave the center as he takes the X. We continue around the circle until everyone has a chance. Central to my actor training, Hello is a diagnostic tool that not only assesses everyone quickly and accurately but lays a firm foundation for the scenes and plays that follow. It establishes a deep connection between scene partners, encouraging intimacy, trust, and the willingness to put instincts ahead of ideas. Although direct and extended eye contact is undesirable, even dangerous in a prison, it is requisite for the exercise to work. The benefits far outweigh the risks in developing acting technique, and in the isolating and hostile environment in which the inmates live, Hello is powerful and poignant in a fundamental way—they are acknowledged, *seen*.

++++

"I don't want to talk about it."

"What?"

"I don't want to talk about it!"

"What don't you want to talk about?"

"Look, I said I didn't want to talk about it, okay?"

"Okay!"

Two of the men are doing a kickass reading of a scene from James McLure's *Private Wars* when Larry says it's time to wind up. I look at the clock and am stunned to see there are only five minutes left. I prepared copiously for the two-and-a-half-hour class and, checking my notes, realize I have only gotten through a third of my prep. Too often, when teaching new students, I find myself moving along quickly from one exercise to the next to hold their attention, skimming the surface and giving an overview rather than an in-depth workout. But these men were so hungry and willing that I worked each exercise and improvisation and scene to the maximum.

Before I leave, each man shakes my hand and thanks me for making the trip. It's clear they appreciated and enjoyed the work, but they seem most grateful for the ninety-minute drive I made, the hours I spent with them.

Exiting the prison is much easier than entering—a cursory look at our bags, a quick scan for the invisible stamp, the return of licenses and keys. As the second hurricane fence slides open and we drive off the grounds and down the road past the miniature castle, I chalk it up to a once-in-a-lifetime experience that will undoubtedly enhance many rehearsals and classes to come.

++++

Larry calls a few months later to say the guys are wondering if I would come back and do it again. The timing is awful. I have no real paying work, auditions are beyond sporadic, my agent is MIA, and advances are not being advanced for the myriad writing projects I am composing and pitching. Not exactly the time to be giving it away. I protest too much, but eventually agree to an encore, with a pointed caveat:

"Just this once."

The second class is standing room only, word of mouth having bumped up the numbers considerably. After Larry reintroduces me, he steps back and watches from the perimeter. I teach them Rhythm, another handclapping and finger-snapping exercise. Again, my fear they might think it childish or girly disappears as they seize the game with vigor. Its 1-2-3-4 rhythm as they call out the numbers designating their place in the circle awakes in everyone the freedom of the playground and the camaraderie of childhood friends. The exercise has a hidden catharsis for the men, which I discover as it plays out. The men's Department Identification Numbers (DINs) are stamped onto their uniforms, often relegating them to a number rather than a name. In Rhythm, the numbers are arbitrary and temporary, defusing the institutional label. As I increase the tempo with each round, the walls fade along with the numbers on their breast pockets.

Gimme is an exercise where one person has something another person needs. I stand "onstage" at one side of the classroom with a plain envelope and ask someone to get it from me. Three guys leap from their chairs ready to assail me before I explain that they cannot use physical force or threats. They must *think* of how to attain their goal—determine *who* I am, *what* is in the envelope, and *why* they need it. Maybe I'm their boss and have their paycheck, or I'm the mailman with an important delivery, or I am a celebrity announcing an Academy Award winner and need ... *the envelope, please.* Once the conditions are satisfied, the envelope must be handed over. The exercise goes well until one of the men refuses to give up the envelope no matter how many petitioners meet the requirements of the ask. When he becomes completely unreasonable, I step in:

"Inmate Walker, everything is set for your release next week. However, if you have not submitted your medical clearance, it will be delayed indefinitely. Is that it there?"

He surrenders the envelope immediately.

After class there is another round of handshakes and heartfelt thank-yous. I wish everyone the best of luck and exit a free man. Or so I think. Walking down the hallway toward the waiting van, with every intention of making a clean getaway, I think of Ernie. I found him as a kitten outside of Ernest Jenkins School in East New York where I was directing a fourth-grade talent show. I had no intention of adopting a kitten that day, but after an affectionate moosh to my chin, found myself walking into the school with Ernie in my arms and asking the hall monitor where I could keep him until I finished rehearsal. Turning to Larry, I do it again:

"So, what do I have to do to be able to come here every week?"

Over the next month I am bonded, fingerprinted, and photographed. I fill out an application, review disclaimers, study rules, sign compliance agreements, and take a tuberculosis test. Once the paperwork is filed and the test results are received, I become an official volunteer at Ferrisburg Correctional Facility. It is an impetuous and life-changing move that ultimately proves that the heart and feet know a hell of a lot more than the head and wallet.

++++

After three months of conducting actor training with the men, I introduce the idea of doing a show for the prison population and some outside guests, pending permission from the Department of Corrections and Community Supervision (DOCCS). As I await DOCCS's decision, I rifle through the massive file of published scenes and monologues I have accrued over the years, selecting what I feel is the strongest and most appropriate material for our first outing. The result is an evening that boasts a wide variety of scenes spanning decades in origin, including one from *Fathers and Sons*, the catalyst for this whole covenant. Shortly after culling together a master script, I receive approval to do three performances for the inmates and visiting civilians.

We call the show *Tuf Love*. Each scene delves into difficult and complex relationships where familial and affectionate bonds are threatened by warring egos and societal conditioning. In the spirit of laying bare these intimate and intense issues, I seat the entire cast onstage, creating a second audience that surrounds the playing area. Set pieces are simple and practical—a table, some cots and chairs, a bench. A backdrop is formed by the inmates' green coats and mesh bags hung on wooden pegs that line the rear wall of the Blue Room, a large empty space adjacent to the gymnasium. I bring in some basic lighting equipment and arrange for a drummer and guitarist from the facility to provide musical segues between the scenes. The honesty of the physical presentation and the astounding progress made by the actors over several months of rehearsal coalesces into a riveting piece of theatre.

The evening is bookended by *The Actor's Vow*, an honest and dramatic statement by Elia Kazan wherein an actor speaks to the honor of the profession, and how each actor's unique qualities and idiosyncrasies are invaluable in portraying a character. Like my teacher and mentor, Gene Frankel, I use Kazan's vow regularly in class, each man personalizing and performing his own version of it for his peers to demonstrate how everyone uses themselves as the instruments they play. In the show, *The Actor's Vow* both introduces and recapitulates the dramatic terrain the men have traversed throughout the show.

Then something happens that will become a sad and regular occurrence at Ferrisburg. I lose an actor shortly before the show opens. Someone shoved Hun Soo in the mess hall, a fight ensued, and Hun Soo has been sent to The Box—solitary confinement—at another prison. Although I plead with my staff advisor to intercede on his behalf, it is beyond her control.

In the late '90s I directed a student production of scenes from classic American plays, including Clifford Odets's *Golden Boy,* at Bayard Rustin High School. I cast Abdalalim, an African immigrant new to the U.S., in the role of Joe Bonaparte, a young boxer and musician. Although he struggled with English, Abdalalim was a natural actor with great instincts who shone onstage. Several of his teachers, concerned about his failing grades and social incompatibility, told me they had never seen him so committed to anything before.

A few days before we were to open, a boy punched Abdalalim's girlfriend in the cafeteria and, naturally, Abdalalim punched him back. He was immediately suspended, jeopardizing the show and devastating Abdalalim. I finagled an appointment with the principal only to be met with an icy stare and a pat line: "Rules are rules."

Turning to leave, I noticed a small pin on the principal's lapel that read "Kids First." It just burst out of me:

"Do you really want to be responsible for taking away the *one thing* this kid has, his chance to feel like he can *do* something in this school, in this country? I'm sure you don't want to hurt him like that. I'm sure you can think of an alternative penalty for his misguided action while still allowing him to hold on to something that is actually *working* for him."

The next day I received word that Abdalalim could perform in the show but would be suspended from classes during the production and the following week. I will never know why the principal changed her mind, but I am grateful to this day that she did.

Unfortunately, I have no one to appeal to on behalf of Hun Soo, no way to even attempt to bring about a resolution. One of the other men steps into his role, and we move forward. It is the first of many challenges and bitter disappointments I will encounter creating theatre behind these walls.

From the moment the first man stands, walks downstage into a small spotlight, and speaks the opening words of the vow—"I will take my rightful place onstage and I will be myself..."—the audience is rapt. During the finale, when everyone proclaims the vow together, their voices overlapping and building to a roar, the applause begins long before the final line is cried in unison: "I WILL BE HEARD!"

My favorite moment in the show is not a dramatic scene or the rousing finale. It is a scene change: a technical shift where a cot is lifted over a row of chairs and placed silently on the floor as a preset for the next scene. Every time I watch the two men in green short-sleeved shirts lift the cot gracefully over their heads and pin-pointedly place it on its spike marks without a sound, I am enthralled. It is a

I am always in awe of the intimacy and tenderness the men are able to demonstrate in a scene or exercise despite the harsh environment in which they live. **Nick Canfield / Courtesy of Stopped Clock Films.**

ballet—beautiful, strong, disciplined. I cannot help thinking that where many might imagine a place like this filled with thugs and brutes, in this gorgeous moment all I see are artists and craftsmen.

The day after the closing performance we meet during our usual class time for a postmortem (and clandestine cast party) to talk about the performance experience. The men spend their meager budgets on Cheez Doodles, sandwich creme cookies, and Crystal Light drink mix from the commissary. I am usually uneasy at parties and social events, the shy nerdy kid reappearing when I no longer have a role to play (the director) and must simply be one among many. But this simple gathering is so warm and inviting that I feel completely at ease.

We laugh about the moments of panic—the lines that were dropped, the light that blew out during the middle of a scene, the PA announcement going off at the absolute wrong time, the puppy-behind-bars who made his stage debut during the finale. Laughter transmutes into tears as several of the men share what this first-time experience was like:

"I never did nothing like this before. I never let nobody... you know... like... *see* me."

They congratulate and thank one another for having each other's backs, for hanging in there during all the trials that came down over the past few months. We lift our Styrofoam cups and make a special toast to Hun Soo. Moze hands me a homemade card from the cast. On the envelope is written, "To *Our* Gene Frankel."

From the very first class, Moze has acted as an ambassador for the Theatre Workshop. He has monitored the callout lists, advocated for new members, and made sure there was hot water for tea and coffee. During the production, he extended his diplomatic duties to the audience, welcoming outside guests as they entered our makeshift performance space, the Blue Room. I treasure the image of Moze escorting my dear friend Mary Bringle, the brilliant and noted novelist, into the "theatre." Mary, with her shocking white hair and dark sunglasses, on the arm of Moze, in his woolen maroon shirt and long dreadlocks, were about as red-carpet as you could get.

A few weeks before the show, on a rehearsal break, Moze says he wants to ask me a question. The room goes silent. This has obviously been a long time coming:

"Rich, how come you come here?"

He pauses, and then goes on:

"'Cause I don't get a *do-gooder* vibe off of you."

It will take me almost a year to answer his question.

2

BROTHERS

Before I placed the first red X on the floor of Room 8 in Building 112 at Ferrisburg CF, I fixed another X in another Room 8—at an Alternative-to-Incarceration in downtown Manhattan. Longtime friend David Rothenberg—founder of the Fortune Society, a New York City–based nonprofit organization that provides support for the formerly incarcerated—had attended the Bayard Rustin production that included the scene from *Golden Boy* and was impressed with the students' performances as well as comments from staff members about never having seen anything like it at Rustin before. David recommended I teach a class at the ATI where he knew the director. I was unfamiliar with this kind of program, a stopgap for young people who have cases pending, allowing them to continue their high school studies and receive counseling and other services in a secure daytime facility in lieu of being held in full-time detention centers. I liked the idea and agreed to give it a shot. During the interview, when asked by the administrator the name of my program, I realized I had never put into words the kind of guerilla theatre I have been doing for years.

Reflecting on some of the chaotic and beautiful moments from past classes and shows, I made a name up on the spot: "Acting Out."

++++

My ATI class consists of fifteen-year-old boys who are awaiting trials that will result in their being released, remanded, or imprisoned. Fear and anger pervade the center; many of the parole officers and attendants have themselves passed through the very system they are now monitoring, and it seems they are not much the wiser or more sensitive for it. Shouting, threatening, browbeating... a lot of literal and figurative "Get out of my sight!" stuff. Just what these kids do not need—they are already well out of the sights of their families, friends, schools, and communities.

Kendrick shows up in class hyper and ready to shake things up. Over the next few weeks, I watch him transform from being wise-cracking and noncooperative to wisecracking and totally down with the work. After a particularly complex exercise in which he excels, he proclaims to the class: "I'm a actor!"

And indeed, he is. As we rehearse for a public presentation of scenes, Kendrick sets the standard for the class: punctual, reliable, committed. He learns his lines before anyone else and always volunteers to stand in for someone who is absent. His parole officer is impressed: "I think Kendrick's found his niche."

He rehearses and performs three scenes. The Mamet and Shepard are terrific, but the Beckett (which he chose himself) is a mountaintop experience. The many luminous productions of *Waiting for Godot* I have seen fade into obscurity as I witness Kendrick's performance in the final moment of Beckett's absurd and existential masterpiece.

Kendrick, playing Estragon, proposes to his classmate Lamar, playing Vladimir, that they end the paucity of their existence by hanging themselves from a tree. Lamar points out that they lack even the means to do that—no rope—and so must keep on living. Sighing, Kendrick looks up at the tree (drawn on butcher paper by the art class), runs his hand over his long cornrows, reaches deep inside and, with the subtlest and saddest smile I have ever seen on a human face, says:

"...True."

He really gets it. But then again, who better to understand Beckett's conundrum of waiting for something that might never come than a teenaged boy expelled from school, branded with a record, and lost in the system? What greater exemplar than a young/old soul who yearns to end the kind of life he is living but lacks the guidance and wherewithal to do it?

A few weeks later, despite his good behavior and outstanding work in the showcase, a judge remands Kendrick to the ATI for an indeterminate time. It crushes him. He never comes back to class.

On a brutal July afternoon, a few months after the end of the term, I receive a call from one of the administrative assistants at the ATI. She informs me that Kendrick has been murdered in his apartment by a member of a rival gang. I stand holding the phone, like a prop in a play, struggling for breath and asking mundane questions about when and where a service will be held.

On the day of Kendrick's wake, I make my way to East New York, Brooklyn, with a totally inadequate card, a hundred dollars in cash, and a copy of *Waiting for Godot* to give to his mother. When I arrive at the funeral home, I am shocked to find no one there except four young girls whispering in the back of the visitation room. I walk up front and sit a few feet from the coffin and weep. For the loss of such a brilliant artist. For the gang colors in which he is dressed. For the lack of attention to the end of his young life. For just about every fucking injustice and tragedy I can think of.

The funeral home director tells me that Kendrick's mother was too shaken to come that afternoon and stayed home, perhaps explaining what kept everyone else away. I obtain her address and with my friend Joe, who has occasionally assisted in class, I make my way to the projects where Kendrick lived. As we walk into the building, we draw stares from all around, doubtless due to our race. Joe remarks impassively, "They think we're cops."

There are hastily reproduced pictures of Kendrick taped up in the lobby with dozens of colored glass candles bunched together on the floor beneath the photos. We ride to the top floor in the poorly maintained and heavily graffitied elevator. More pictures and candles line the hallway leading to the apartment.

I ring the bell and wait. A dog barks angrily inside and there is a lot of shouting about removing him to another room. When a young girl finally opens the door and I explain who I am, she leads us inside. There are several vases of arranged flowers around the room and the dining room table is laden with bowls and plates and pans of food. The walls of the apartment are lined with white plastic folding chairs. For all intents and purposes, *this* is where the wake is being held. The girl nods toward a youngish, heavyset woman across the room. Kendrick's mother rises from one of the folding chairs and walks toward me. Standing several feet from the doorway in which Kendrick was shot and killed, she avoids my eyes as I hand her the card. I point to the cover of the play and struggle to tell her how brilliant her son was in the scene from *Godot*. I echo his parole officer in saying how he found his niche, though dare not say what we both know: that it was not in time.

I extol his artistry and talent, but she is unable to take it in, locked behind a wall of grief and staring over my shoulder into an unforgiving future. It is not until I tell her how Kendrick seemed to see things that others did not—*could* not—see, that she looks in my eyes for the first time. Her face brightens as she recognizes me—not as someone she knows, but someone who knows what her boy knew. Our embrace is sudden, mutual. We hold each other and cry. She whispers in my ear:

"Yes. Yes, he could. He could always see so much more."

I suspect we all can—if we dare, if we allow ourselves to see. If we remove the blinders and the defenses, the need to react, to be right, to save face, to win. If we stop punishing and start helping. If we realize that there are solutions to a lot of the suffering and misunderstanding that drive people to do things they really do not want to do. That those solutions can be found in art and music and dance and theatre. That those things set us right. That expressing ourselves creatively is something we need to do to be fully human.

++++

I was seventeen and only had my driver's license for little over a month when I had a fender bender. I knew my father would go off on me, and he did. His attack was so humiliating that I tore up my license. Then he did something that seemed even more cruel than reaming me out for crashing his car. He picked up the pieces of my license, handed them to me, and told me to go to the store for milk. When I said I could not, would not, he physically pushed me out the door. He said if I did not drive right away, I might never again. Albeit from the mouth of a brute, it turned out to be wise advice.

David Rothenberg reaffirms that counsel after my work at the ATI. He sees how shaken I am after Kendrick's murder and notices I am slowly backing away from the work I love. In his decades with The Fortune Society, David has seen it all. There had been much anguish along the way, and times when I'm sure *he* wanted to get out of the line of fire. But he never did. And he is not going let me, either.

I receive a call from the program director at Fortune, who needs a teacher for a group of young parolees. David has told her about my Acting Out class and she feels it is just what they are looking for. The men, ranging in age from late teens to mid-twenties, are studying for their GEDs and trying to get back on their feet after having their lives interrupted by jail sentences. I tell the director I'll think about it. I call David with a million reasons why I am not ready. He is implacable: "Richard, just do it."

I know he's right. And I trust him. So, I tape my proverbial license together once again and get back behind the wheel. I'm still apprehensive when I arrive for my first class at Fortune's new flagship building in the industrial wilds of Queens, but I am pleased with the manageable class size, the enthusiasm of the group, and the ubiquitous Blue Room (an apparent mainstay in these institutions) to which I am assigned. X marks the spot once again and a three-month residency begins. Sixteen guys consistently show up to class, respond well to the exercises, and are enthusiastic about performing for an invited audience at the end of the term.

A few weeks into class, two boys named Mathias and Kendrick (an oddly comforting coincidence) show up early, in the middle of a heated argument. They accost me, trying to beat each other to the punch, one calling my name louder than the other and pushing to the front of a nonexistent line. When Mathias finally concedes, Kendrick comes out with it:

"Rich... we want to ask you something and you have to answer the truth, okay?"

I assume it has something to do with class or the upcoming show—who is being cast in what role or will there be agents and theatre professionals attending. Judging from their fervor, I suspect it might even be a case of who is doing a better job. I am completely unprepared for Kendrick's question:

"Would you rather be stabbed or shot?"

By the look on their faces, I can see this is not a time for speeches about conflict resolution, or rhetoric on violence and its rippling effect on society. Nor is it a time to wax eloquent on art and life and the universe. It is a time for a reply. I think about it for a few seconds:

"Shot."

Kendrick jumps up and down, screaming with glee:

"See, I told you! I told you!"

Even years afterward, I will have no idea why Kendrick is so thrilled that he is right or why it matters in the first place. Nevertheless, once *that* is settled, we can get on with our work. I have learned that most young people do not want their questions analyzed or judged— they just want them answered.

I make one whopping mistake during the residency at Fortune that almost jeopardizes the project. A scene from Odets's *Paradise Lost* requires a gun. I buy a cheap water pistol, paint it black, and throw it into a bag with the rest of the props without running it by the administration. There is an age-old rule in the theatre forbidding actors to touch anyone else's props lest they are lost or misplaced when needed. My actors follow the rule diligently, but that does not prevent Malik from taking *his* prop, the water gun (from a distance indistinguishable from the real thing), and, during a break in rehearsal, walking into his counselor's office and pointing it at her as "a joke."

I am called into the program director's office and ripped a new one. She asks me what I was thinking and, before I can answer, tells me I was not thinking at all. I stand there like a penitent child. I have no defense. I not only screwed up, I broke one of my own directives, something I tell every actor before we start working together: *Don't ever forget where you are and why you are there.*

In my zeal for authenticity, I forgot that guns are the objects that almost destroyed the lives of many of these young men, and that weapons have no place in the work we do. I forgot that the imagination of the actor and the audience is far more powerful than any hand prop called for in a play. I forgot my responsibility as their teacher and guide. And I forgot the tenet of one of my idols, Bertolt Brecht, who went out of his way to remind audiences that what they were watching was not real—only the message was.

After that, when a weapon is required in a show, we use wooden blocks or sensory objects. We suggest rather than substantiate. We adjust the parameters of the scene so that threats may be posed without the actual instrument of that threat. And with today's oversaturation of guns in news, film, and everyday life, it is not only a revolutionary

move, but also a not-so-subtle reminder of the power of art and imagination over force and violence.

++++

Kendrick and Mathias have been working on the same *Waiting for
Godot* scene from the ATI, which I had originally cut from the lineup
out of some vague notion of respect for the young man who appeared
in it earlier, and now have reinstated for the same reason. These two
lads could not be more perfectly matched to the scene: their constant
wacky philosophical arguments (which clearly entail preferred methods
of being snuffed) as well as their fierce loyalty to each other at this difficult time in their lives allow them to effortlessly deliver the goods.
Although they are in their early twenties, you can easily imagine them
sitting out in front of a bodega playing dominoes with the rest of the
viejos in the neighborhood. And that's how I direct the scene.

Mathias's counselor tells me that Acting Out is the first class he
has really participated in. In fact, it is the first time he has ever *spoken*
in class. His MO has been a lot of head nodding and grunting, but
here he is, not only speaking but standing onstage and giving voice
to Beckett's Vladimir with a cogency that is impressive. Kendrick is
the opposite—mercurial, cagey, never missing a dramatic beat. The
combination of their disparate rhythms is hypnotic. You don't doubt
them for a second.

In addition to the Beckett, I choose a variety of published scenes
that depict fiery personal relationships between male family members
and friends. We call the show *Brothers,* and each scene plumbs the
depths of these fraternal relationships, aptly closing with Mathias and

Kendrick in *Godot*. Kendrick makes it all too real when, at the final performance, a dentist appointment delays his arrival. Our communal relief is palpable as he runs in at the last moment and steps into the scene just as it is about to start. Mathias says we should have called the scene "Waiting for Kendrick."

One piece causes a stir—the opening of *Answers,* a one-act play by Tom Topor, in which two detectives grill a man about an unspecified crime he may or may not have committed. The interrogation is intentionally over the top, designed to break down the suspect and compel him to confess to the crime regardless of his culpability. It mirrors events in the lives of many of these young men, intensified by racial profiling and abject bigotry. The real-life cast would most likely consist of a suspect who was a young person of color being interrogated by two older white police officers. I decide to turn it on its head and bring in an older Caucasian colleague to play the suspect and cast two of my

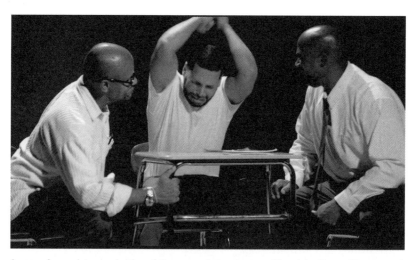

A scene from a later production of the one-act play *Answers.* Two detectives grill a suspect, the actors all too familiar with the harrowing territory. **Nira Burstein / Courtesy of Stopped Clock Films.**

guys, both African American, as the cops. When the lights fade up on a couple of young black cops grilling an old white guy, the audience is mesmerized before anyone says a word. It is quite a departure from ubiquitous TV shows and movies, and it sets up a flashpoint of emotions from the start.

The challenge has been to keep my actors from imitating what they have seen (and experienced firsthand), to bring their unique perspective to the scene rather than merely settling for artistic retribution. Although the play *does* demonstrate an unsympathetic demeanor on the part of the officers, I have urged the men to dig deeper: even if their characters are willing participants in the system, they can try and subtly buck that system to see what happens.

The result is fascinating. Instead of exacting revenge or stereotyping themselves, they sidestep clichés and transcend the expected. There is certainly an ominous edge, but since they can identify with the position of the suspect more than the cops, there is also a compassion that hums beneath the playwright's uncharitable stage directions. It is as if the audience is on the other side of the two-way glass and the young men have agreed to show them the power they *could* wield without doing so.

I have always been uncomfortable describing people by race. I think it is one of the most divisive brandings in our society. But after decades of working with inner-city youth in impoverished neighborhoods—and, later, with the incarcerated—I am all too sadly aware that most of my students in these dire situations are people of color. Yet, despite this seemingly impossible predicament, I have found that theatre is a temporary panacea, ameliorating the imbalance briefly by providing opportunities for marginalized people to walk in someone else's shoes, assume other social roles, and portray characters onstage that they are prevented from playing in life. Inhabiting these roles and filling these spaces awakens something in the actor, in the *person*: an awareness that they are capable of more than is expected of them, that they do not have to surrender to the status quo even if their current circumstances speak to the contrary. I tell my students all the time: "Acting is not about being someone else, it's about being *you*. And the beauty of it is that *you* can be *anybody*."

At the *Brothers* cast party, David Rothenberg pulls me aside: "Look."

I follow his gaze and we both watch the guys swiping slices of pizza, pouring each other sodas, micro-hugging, backslapping, and laughing about the close calls and dropped lines—*laughing* about the mistakes they made, and freely forgiving themselves and each other. David shakes his head in awe: "A few months ago, they would not even make eye contact."

3

INSIDE OUT

Ten months after Moze asks me his not-so-rhetorical question, the same hush reigns over the room in Ferrisburg as I answer him. Appropriately, I am standing on the X in the center of the floor:

"I come here because this is one of the most vibrant and talent-filled rooms in which I have ever worked. And the reason I don't seem like a do-gooder is because, with all the mistakes I have made in my life, being in the wrong place at the wrong time, doing the wrong thing more times than I care to admit, I could very well be sitting here in state greens myself... as I daresay could many others."

There are no gasps or protests or cries of disbelief. They know the truth when they hear it. Many of the men were arrested and jailed when they were kids—damaged, confused, trying to survive in impossible neighborhoods and dysfunctional families, trapped by addiction, aching to find something they could call their own. They ran with the wrong people, did questionable things, and got in trouble with the law. Unspoken, though obvious, is the fact that my complexion and college degree saved my ass more than a few times, receiving a pass or fine or slap on the wrist in lieu of an indictment. We never discuss it again, but I sense they are grateful I said it, that someone said it.

After *Tuf Love*, we fold in some new men and I resume teaching a straight acting class, continuing to strengthen skills and hone technique. I introduce more complex exercises that demand greater physical dexterity, mental acuity, and emotional risk-taking. The Hello exercise moves beyond one-liners to two, three, and four lines of dialogue.

"I want to go back."
"To where?"
"Before it happened."
"I'm with you, brother."

The power of the micro-scenes occurring in the center of the room galvanizes our work. I encourage the men go with what happens rather than plan anything out, to explore what is already there.

"I think I'm gonna cry."
"What happened?"
"Life happened."
"Go ahead, I got you."

After a few months of steady progress, it is time to get back out on the boards. I have no plans for a specific show, so I put it to the men. Hector, who has served as my stage manager, assistant director, and right-hand man over the past year, quiets the room and reps the company:

"We want to do the same thing we did last time, only we want to write it ourselves."

I shift gears and designate the first ninety minutes of class a writing workshop where the men either create new scenes and monologues or edit work they have already written. I draw on exercises I used when conducting writing workshops on Rikers. Place is a strong catalyst for the men. One of the prompts is to write about a physical or psychological place where they spent either the best or worst time in their lives. It elicits a lot of material around incarceration—what it was like before, what happened, what it is like now, and how they imagine their lives after release. In another exercise they write to, about, or *as* a person they love, hate, or are worried about. Their letters and visits and phone calls fill their loose-leaf pages. As the show takes shape, so does the title: *Inside Out.*

The pieces vary wildly: political spoken-word rants, hilarious jailhouse romps, tense cop stakeouts, bizarre dream sequences, poignant letters home. One of the most unusual pieces is written in Spanish, translated into English, performed in both languages, and choreographed as a stark ballet expressing the loneliness of solitary confinement. Two of the guys compose a song to open and close the show:

I'm hurting on the inside
I'm looking at the outside
Praying for another chance
To change a wrong and make it right...

Once the pieces are finished, read, polished, and placed in tentative order for the evolving production, we return to actor training and move into rehearsal. Hector suggests I procure binders for everyone's script, as the stapled versions used during *Tuf Love* were constantly lost or damaged. Locating binders without metal parts (which are disallowed by DOCCS) is a challenge. I scour the internet and find an all-plastic, three-ring binder made by a company in China. Hector is thrilled with this very official and practical device, affectionally referring to it as *his* iPad. It is gratifying and touching to watch the men arrive with their official scripts under their arms or in their netted bags. Hector's idea is spot-on. Not only do the binders preserve the scripts, but they also lend a professional quality to rehearsals and bump up everyone's ownership of the project.

Forgiveness is more than a recurring theme in *Inside Out*; it is an undercurrent than runs throughout. When a theatre colleague once asked what compelled me to work with the incarcerated, I found the answer as it passed my lips: "I identify with their need to be forgiven."

It is an involuntary response to a life-altering event that is impossible for me to remember. I spent the first year and a half of my life in foster care after my mother suffered a debilitating nervous breakdown and was hospitalized. I was placed in care because the warring factions of my family were unwilling to concede custody to either side. It may be just psychological theorizing, but I suspect that their clinical and insensitive solution left me feeling that I was somehow responsible, that there was something wrong with *me*. I have struggled with this feeling most of my life. I sometimes feel a similar vibe permeating the room.

Inside Out heightens perceptions considerably as to guilt and innocence, justice and injustice. Rather than looking away, we intensify those perceptions in the rehearsal process. Dropping their defenses, the men find the courage to step into the light as they are—warts and neuroses and criminal behavior and all.

++++

There was a room at the high school academy in the South Bronx where I taught for a few years called the Safe Room. It was where kids who misbehaved were sent to cool their heels, a kind of in-house suspension or detention during school hours. Marcus, one of the boys who was often in trouble, seemed to spend more time in the Safe Room than in class. He told me the only reason he came to school was when he remembered he had acting class. Marcus loved acting because he could vent without getting in trouble or hurting anyone. One day in rehearsal, he was spellbound by an explosive and confrontational scene played out by two of the other boys. Afterward, when the actors high-fived each other, thrilled with what they had accomplished, Marcus proclaimed:

"*This* is the *real* safe room!"

It's how I've come to think of the Theatre Workshop—a place where the men can be who they are and feel what they feel despite being surrounded by twenty-foot walls and around-the-clock surveillance.

When the men ask me to contribute a piece to the show, I write a scene of reconciliation based on a short film I saw years ago that had a lasting effect. In "But for the Grace," a father visits the young man who killed his daughter in a drunk driving accident.

I apologized twelve years ago when it happened and at every single hearing since. I apologized so many times to so many people in so many ways, but I don't even think my own mother can ever forgive me for what I did. And no matter how many times I say I'm sorry and no matter how sorry I really am, that won't bring your daughter back.

Making mistakes, having regrets, wishing one did things differently. *Inside Out* is filled with these battles of conscience, and the men are undaunting in their attempt to forgive themselves, each other, and those who caused *them* harm. It is reconstituting and goes a long way in helping me to reckon *my* mistakes, the reckless actions I took in my youth, the addictions I fed, the people I hurt. In watching these men learn to move past some of the painful events of their lives, I become capable of doing the same. It is not why I do this work, but the ancillary effect is undeniable. And it is not just past trauma that these men are learning to resolve—it is also the day-to-day humiliations of prison life that further compound their struggle to right themselves in

An earlier version of "But for the Grace" in *Inside Out* where the father breaks down while confessing his crime to the man responsible for his daughter's death. **Brent Buell.**

what must seem like a very wrong world. Before rehearsal one day I see, through the wire mesh windows of the transport van, one of my most ardent actors up against the side of a truck being frisked as his comrades walk by, eyes trained forward, grateful it is not them. It is sobering to know that the defenses he must put up during and after the frisk will have to be dropped shortly afterward at workshop for an emotional monologue in which he speaks to his loneliness and regret. I am amazed by his ability to negotiate these two highly charged states while retaining his dignity and drive to continue.

Choosing a set for *Inside Out* is challenging because of the rapid scene changes and wide range of locations and storylines. Once, while directing Random House's annual award ceremony at Symphony Space, I found a sturdy, malleable, and lightweight solution for an evening of multifarious performance pieces: black plastic milk crates. Getting Random House to loan us the crates was easy; having seventy-two of them cleared by the prison is a whole other production. The deputy of security, in a heated meeting, feels that the sheer amount of milk crates being brought into the facility is a security issue. I imagine inmates creating a huge stair unit out of the crates and traipsing over a plastic mountain to freedom like in *The Sound of Music*. The deputy of security's main argument is that it will be difficult to see inside so many crates. The superintendent bursts into laughter:

"What the hell, Pete... like an inmate is going to hide *inside* one?"

My relief at receiving permission to bring in the milk crates is soon tempered by the realization that, because of my one-man-band status, *I* must hand carry all seventy-two crates from my truck to the arsenal, the arsenal to the van, the van to the gym... and, of course, when the show closes, all the way back.

Inside Out enjoys a lighting upgrade thanks to Mike Abrams, with whom I worked for years at Random House and is now my regular lighting designer. He fashions a simple and highly functional light board constructed from household dimmers and plug boxes that can handle the aggregate power of our modest equipment: industrial flood lights and birdies, tiny spotlights used for special moments. Hundreds of yards of cable, another security nightmare, run from the board to various outlets spread throughout the Blue Room. With our new set and lighting upgrades, we successfully convert The Blue Room into a semi-legitimate Black Box theatre, which the men now call the Black-and-Blue Room. A third color dominates the space—gel #327, a deep forest green Gene Frankel superstitiously demanded be included somewhere in the light plot of every production he directed. The guys like the idea of summoning *my* director in this way and it certainly comforts me to have him around in spirit.

A therapist tries to intervene when two psychiatric prison patients come to blows over a bummed cigarette in the hilarious "G Building" in *Inside Out*. **Brent Buell.**

Inside Out turns out to be a panoply of compact scenes and monologues that shed an alternately harsh and absurd light on incarceration. The program headings read like a hip-hop libretto: *Wake Up, Smoke and Mirrors, His-Story, Random Thoughts, The Incident, The Letter, Here, Shadows, A Series of Ones...* The evening closes with a piece Drew wrote called *The Dilemma,* which imagines his upcoming parole hearing. He has created a character named Davis who recounts the brutal childhood that placed him (Davis *and* Drew) on an inevitable path to crime and imprisonment. Toward the end of *The Dilemma,* when the commissioners ask Davis for a personal statement, he not only expresses his deep and sincere remorse for his crime but exhibits a fundamental shift in identity. Like so many in the workshop, he is clearly not the same man who committed the crime; rather, he is someone who has exorcised his demons and risen above the oppressive environment in which he now lives. He is a man making proper amends, who plans to be a leader in the community by helping young people avoid the perils that befell him. (After leaving prison, Drew will go on to run an urban youth program with an anti-gun and anti-crime agenda.)

It is almost a perfect finale, but I feel it needs fortifying, more manpower—something we certainly have in abundance. Since most of the men in the cast come from similar, often nearly identical, backgrounds and have committed comparable crimes, I propose creating a chorus that echoes Davis's story, each man adding his unique statistics and making it *everyone's* story. Drew is open to the idea and the adjustment creates a unified front with greater impact. Davis/Drew leads the chorus with aplomb:

DAVIS

In no way is this a justification for my actions. But the facts are that I grew up in a home that would be considered...

CHORUS

...Dysfunctional.

DAVIS

Both my parents were into drugs and violence. One of my first memories is the two of them fighting over a crack pipe...

CHORUS

... A forty ... A blunt ... A TV show ... ten bucks ... Something stupid ...

DAVIS

My mother ended up with two black eyes and a broken nose. I was about eight...

CHORUS

... seven ... five ... nine ... six ... ten ...

DAVIS

That was my first lesson that violence was the answer to every-thing. I was the oldest of three...

CHORUS

... The youngest of nine ... The middle child ... The only step-child ... In foster care ... The oldest of thirteen ...

At the end of *The Dilemma*, the men line up onstage and, one by one, speak aloud the years of their actual prison sentences while standing in front of a huge wall of crates lit eerily to look like the outside gates of the prison. Many of the cast are serving life sentences and after the numbered sentences are announced, the lifers begin their chilling litany:

"Life."

"Life."

"Life."

"Life."

"Life."

"Life…"

Then comes the line that closes the play, an all-too-familiar phrase that is the cue for inmates to begin moving back to their cells or dorms: "On the Go Back!" It is shouted over walkie-talkies and down hallways by COs at the end of classes, work shifts, twelve-step meetings, rec periods, chow times, and visits. In the play, as my sound operator parrots that line over our jerry-rigged sound system (a boom box fed through two microwave-size speakers) the cast marches slowly behind the huge wall of crates and reprises the opening song:

I'm hurting on the inside…
I'm looking at the outside…

The dirge has a visceral effect on the shaken audience members, who are now reeling from a ninety-minute emotional roller-coaster ride. They have not just gotten a glimpse of life behind prison walls; they have felt it.

Drew's actual parole hearing is held the week after the show closes. Later, he shares with us how he kept bugging out during the hearing, feeling as if he were momentarily transported back to the staged version of the proceedings, how he had to constantly remind himself that he was now at the real thing. Drew found that his familiarity with the emotional terrain he negotiated in the play calmed and centered him throughout his actual hearing and he could deftly deflect some of the jabs thrown at him by the commissioners. Most importantly, Drew did not feel alone. In *The Dilemma,* everyone had gone through the hearing with him, and he felt the lingering presence and support of his fellow cast members on that crucial afternoon. He made parole.

Once, leading a high school writing workshop on Rikers Island, I noticed one of the boys staring at the scratched and smeared plexiglass window that framed the south wall of the room, unable to see outside and unable to write. When I approached him, he broke down:

"I just want to get out of here! You don't know what it's like! You don't know!"

I sat next to him for a while, waiting for him to come up for air. Then, as kindly as I could, I told him to try to *write himself out.* I explained that there was a way of leaving a place without actually leaving, and that relief could be found in transferring his thoughts and feelings onto paper, that art could do that for him. In Drew's case, it may have even swung open the gate.

For the first time in my work at Ferrisburg, through a special arrangement with DOCCS, *Inside Out* is attended by the families of the men. The room teems with emotion, rivaling the intensity of the show. Wives, parents, siblings, and children see their husbands, sons, brothers, and fathers in a new light. They witness the men facing fears, taking risks, and performing laudable acts in which they not only succeed, but triumph. Experiencing the inmates, their families, and the other guests engaging in meaningful dialogue after the show is a glimpse into a world for which I have always longed—one where people identify with, listen to, and look for the best in each other.

The night after closing, back in Room 8, we hold the postmortem for *Inside Out*, resplendent with family-size bags of Cheez Doodles, the ubiquitous Crystal Lite, and a disastrously delicious coconut layer cake. I anticipate the wrap-up will be more potent than usual because of the original material and the families having seen the performance. There are the usual laughs about flubs and gaffes during the run, but the sharing becomes serious and emotional in short order. The men are struck by the audience's response, how several of the outside guests wept while thanking them for what they had *done*. They were also affected when other inmates told them how proud they were of them and taken aback when several correctional officers lauded their performances.

Clay is a college student in the City University of New York's college-in-prison program at Ferrisburg, and one of his essays has been selected this year for publication in a collection of work by incarcerated students. In it he describes a horrific event he experienced as a child, when his father ground a lit cigarette into his hand to *make a man* out of him after he was bullied and came home crying. It has given me insight into Clay's hateful and offensive tattoos and his obsession to win every theatre game at any cost. When it is his turn to share, Clay describes how a lot of men stopped him in the yard to tell him how good he was in the show. Tears fill his eyes and his voice breaks:

"Nobody ever told me I did *nothin'* good before. Not in real life."

The unspoken *Amens* fill the room. I look around and realize that these men could very well be the kids in the South Bronx academy or the ATI acting class or the PSY-7 workshop. These *are* the at-risk kids who have fulfilled that ominous prophecy, kids that no one ever acknowledged or complimented or regarded. Kids who, tragically, when they *were* finally noticed, spent decades behind bars. God's kids.

Jake shares last. Six months before, he had been dragged to the workshop by a buddy. Over time he stepped up, let down his guard, and became one of the finest actors in the troupe. In *Tuf Love*, Jake and his buddy played the Loman brothers from *Death of a Salesman*. Jake exposed a life truth of his own when, as Biff, he turned to his brother Happy and blurted:

"Why does Dad mock me all the time... Everything I say there's a twist of mockery on his face. I can't get near him."

In the workshop, Jake has gone from lurking on the edge and sneering at everyone to standing stage center and embracing a new experience with poise and humility. In *Inside Out,* his shining moment is a monologue in which he writes a letter to his mother, apologizing for letting her down and begging her forgiveness. Jake was raised by a foster mother who was anything but loving, which has made his sincere and affectionate performance even more remarkable. At the postmortem, when his time comes to share, he goes mute. He stares at everyone, smiles strangely, and then makes a sound I have never heard before—an unnatural sound, or perhaps an exceedingly natural one, like a wounded animal or a falling tree. He is crying, it seems for the first time as a grown man, and he doesn't know how to do it. Two of the guys walk him out into the hall where he continues making the sound until it slowly transforms into something more familiar, until he starts to learn how to feel something he has never felt before.

I have always been a crier. Sentimental movies, musical theatre, animal rescue commercials—they all take me down. In the comment section of my kindergarten report card, the teacher wrote, "Richard is a very bright boy, but he cries at the drop of a hat." Some things never change. I am amazed at the tears that are shed in classes and shows and postmortems. Certainly not what I expected in a medium security prison: how it clears the air, and bonds us.

When Jake returns, he is laughing and joking and soon fighting over the last piece of coconut cake. We sign each other's programs, inhale sugar and salt, and wring the last drops of coffee from a newly acquired urn on which is scrawled "THEATRE WORKSHOP" in Magic Marker. At nine o'clock, the CO taps on the door and I gather my things. We walk en masse up the hallway, slowly, holding onto the show, to the alternate reality in which we have lived for the past few days. It is not until I climb into the van, and hear the real "On the Go Back!" usher the men out onto the road and up the hill, that it is over. A show closing is always bittersweet. On the inside it is like saying goodbye to the best streak of luck you ever had.

During tech rehearsals, there was a huge snowstorm. I am rarely deterred by weather, having lived in western Michigan's snow belt for five years. I am much like the proverbial postal service when it comes to getting to rehearsal and so, on the day of the storm, I set off for the prison with plenty of time to spare. Unplowed roads and timid drivers clogged the way, and the usual thirty-minute drive from the cottage where I was staying that night took almost two hours. At the gate, the

The cast and crew of *Inside Out* after a successful run in the "Black and Blue Room." **Brent Buell.**

guard was so flabbergasted that I showed up in the storm that he waved me through without checking my ID or documenting my plates. All the time I was being processed in the arsenal and riding in the van to the program area, I anticipated how blown away everyone would be that I made the trek.

As we pulled up to Building 112, I saw Hector standing outside smoking a cigarette and making notes on his clipboard. I jumped out of the van with a flair, ready to receive my hero's welcome. He looked up stoically and grunted:

"You're late."

4

I OF THE STORM

One of the standout and stand-alone pieces in *Inside Out* is a seven-minute explosion of acerbic wit and showmanship called "Acting in Concert." It has spawned from the exercise in which the men wrote about a place they either loved or hated. Billy chose both and wrote about a place he loved to hate. Before serving his fourteen-year sentence upstate, Billy spent a lot of time in holding cells, or bullpens, overcrowded cages with a vast array of characters jockeying for space and status while pleading their cases to self-appointed jailhouse lawyers or anyone who would listen. Chaotic, frightening, depressing, absurd... a rich environment for plumbing by the deft dramatist Billy is proving to be. Aside from his sharp and incisive writing, Billy is a versatile actor with a knack for mimicking idiosyncratic behaviors and an excellent ear for accents, dialects, and speech patterns.

The first time he presents the piece to the class, we are on the floor, howling, gripping our stomachs, begging him to stop and then start again. Afterward, I walk up to him, put my hand on his shoulder, and make a vow:

"If you can give me an hour of that, we will *do* something with it when you get out."

Billy is set to be released in six months and gets right to work. In the meantime, during the run of *Inside Out*, he kills the seven-minute segment:

> So I walks up in the courtroom, right? I walks up in the court-room. I'm like, yo, ya honor, you know what I'm sayin? This is before they even start the proceedings. But he know me, he's like, yo, what up. I'm like, yo, ya honor, D.A.s and them ain't got no muddafuckin lab report. So he like, yo, D.A.s and them? They like, yo, what up. He like, where the muddafuckin' lab report? They like, we ain't got it. But we gon' get it. We gon' get it. So ya know. He kinda lean back in his chair, right? He lookin at me an shit, noddin, so I leans back noddin and shit. Cause he know I know my shit. So he like, ayo, cut that man loose. D.A.s an them like, nah, we gon' get it, we need more time and he like tick, tick, tick, times up. Cut that man loose. Moral of da story: Gotta do your research. Research is when you look for something, can't find it, so you gotta look again.

Every night the audience goes insane, inmates and outside guests screaming wildly, *Oh No*-ing and *No, He Didn't*-ing themselves sick as Billy skewers the penal system and lampoons its real-life cast of characters. It takes more than a few minutes and some extended transition music for the audience to compose themselves after his riff so that the show can indeed go on.

What is remarkable about the material and his performance is that, despite his unforgiving indictment of an institution in dire need of reform, he never sacrifices the humanity of his characters, even those on the other side of the bars.

A few weeks after the performance, Billy hands me the requested hour-long version of the show. It's terrific. Not only is the material smart and audacious, but it has a beginning, middle, and end— something increasingly rare in a lot of solo work. I start coming in an hour earlier on Fridays to rehearse the show, which Billy has retitled *I Am Them*. We work out some minor kinks in the writing, strengthen the closing, and then start staging the piece. I pitch the show to my friend and colleague Robin Hirsch, who runs the Cornelia Street Café in the West Village. Robin is enthusiastic about presenting *I Am Them* at the café when Billy gets out. We book a date, confident that with several months of rehearsal and prep on the inside, we can easily transfer it to Cornelia Street after his release.

I walk into rehearsal one day to find Billy and the two guys who have been assisting with rehearsals sitting glumly on the windowsill. Billy has just been notified he is being transferred to another prison closer to his hometown in preparation for his release. As a volunteer for DOCCS, I am not allowed to have any contact with Billy once he is moved. Calls, letters, discussions, script adjustments, rehearsal plans are verboten—all work on the show must stop. It feels like one of those moments in *Law & Order* when the metallic gavel sound signifies an irrevocable plot change. I experience another one-step-closer-one-step-back glimpse of what it must be like for someone or something to have total control over your life. I call Robin and ask for an indefinite postponement. He graciously complies, assuring us a spot when we are ready.

A few months later, I receive a call from an unknown number. A wild man is ranting unintelligibly. I am just about to hang up when I realize it is one of the characters from Billy's show.

I shout, "Billy!"

He shouts back, "I'm out! I'm out!"

What follows is not an invitation, but a summons to his family home *that* evening for supper. Neither Billy nor his mother will accept anything but an unqualified Yes. I am instructed to bring the script of *I Am Them* that I retyped and imported into my playwriting software. Billy does not want to waste any more time.

I drive out to New Jersey for an authentic Armenian meal and a warm welcome from Billy's immediate and extended family. The food is amazing and extensive... manti, gata, lula kabobs, pilaf, tabbouleh, and a startling abundance of fresh pomegranate seeds. During the feast I can sense his parents' trepidation over what seems to them a fantastical plan to mount his show in New York City. Billy's hell-bent, almost reckless attitude heightens their concerns. A few weeks later, when we share some of the work with his folks at a rehearsal and they see just how damned good the show is and how brilliant he is in it, they get on board and cheer us on.

When I show a video clip of *I Am Them* to David Rothenberg, he is bowled over. David is an avid sports fan and says Billy's hilarious baseball jargon segment brings Abbott and Costello screaming into the twenty-first century.

PYSA: Dari Yeter, de shorosto fo de jankee, fut dut fo dat jear

BILLY: I didn't understand what he said. I don't speak Spanish.

VINNIE: That's English. He's Dominican. He said Derek Jeter, the
shortstop for the Yankees, is fucked up this year. He's injured.

BILLY: Say it again. Slow.

PYSA: Dari Yeter.

BILLY: Derek Jeter.

PYSA: Do shorosto for de jankee.

BILLY: The shortstop for the Yankees

PYSA: Fut dut dat jear.

BILLY: He's fucked up this year. That's amazing, he did say that!

David sets up a performance at The Fortune Society's Castle Gardens in Harlem and obtains some rehearsal space for us at their Long Island City facility. In the meantime, Billy's father arranges for us to work in the large event room above a friend's hookah bar in New Jersey. It's an odd venue, but its proximity to Billy's home is a plus, giving us ample time to work within the confines of his parole curfew.

My son, Jonathan, and Billy's brother, Edward, soon join the team. Although they are supposed to be assisting in rehearsals, they are often useless while holding book during run-throughs. Whenever Billy gets lost and calls "Line!" my hysterical assistants cannot locate the cue, or even the page, everything blurred by tears of laughter. Every evening, after rehearsal, we retire downstairs to the hookah bar's adjoining restaurant, where another incredible meal is served in lieu of a director's fee.

We perform the show at the Cornelia Street Café to a capacity crowd with David Rothenberg front and center. A few weeks later, Billy is strutting his stuff at the Castle Gardens. Due to popular demand, David arranges ongoing monthly performances at the Castle where a theatrical producer, Eric Krebs, catches the show. Eric knows a hit when he sees one, puts his money where his mouth is, and offers us a run at his small Off-Broadway theatre in Times Square. Retitled *Holding* at David's suggestion, the show runs for over a year, garnering rave reviews and notices. The *New York Times* gushes. *Time Out New York* writes a love letter:

> The first time you see a performer as blazingly gifted… you may wonder: Where has this guy been? In this case, there's an answer. Less than a year ago, he was released from prison, where he had served 12 years for assault. Now 35, he has written a comedic solo show inspired by his experience after getting arrested…. The result is astonishing… the thrill of watching a natural talent get sprung on the world.

During its midtown run, *Holding* also makes special appearances at a variety of places around the New York metropolitan area, tickling and thrilling audiences wherever it is presented. But nothing compares with the homecoming Billy receives when he performs the show back at Ferrisburg—the scene of the sentence for the crime. It is a triumphant return—hope and pride and laughter explode from the prison population as they celebrate one of their own who has not only made it out but, in their eyes, *made it.*

David and Eric pull strings and a *New York Times* reporter and photographer are granted permission to come inside to document the unique event. The media attention completely alters the sometimes dismissive and disruptive demeanor of the correctional officers and prison officials. They are at a loss as to how to respond—a positive light is being shed on their institution and it is an *inmate* who is doing it! To date, the superintendent has not attended any of the Theatre Workshop's shows, but when she saunters into the room for *Holding* with several deputies in tow, I know we have turned a corner. (To her credit, she goes on to attend every show thereafter.) The *Times* article is impressive—even kind of surreal, considering the humble beginnings of the show in the Friday-night workshop. Comments from the men who witness the return engagement are quoted in the article and attest to the distance the piece has come:

"You can see the maturity, the process."
"One thing that wasn't evident before was the
    humanity, the tragicomedy of it."
"The characters are not just caricatures."
"It not only reminds us what we can do.... It also
    reminds us not to give up on ourselves."
"We all have our own talents. Billy's a symbol
    of how to use those talents."
"He serves as an example for any inmate who wants to
    succeed on the outside.... The biggest thing is a willingness,
    one's own determination to come out better."

Kudos and testimonials aside, I learn a hard lesson during the process of rehearsing and directing *Holding*. Billy has an extraordinary gift, but without proper training, technique, and professional support in other areas, that gift is undermined. I sense during tech rehearsals that Billy has reached a saturation point with taking notes. Consequently, in previews, he begins straying from the established blocking and changing the pacing when an audience does not give him what he wants. When I call him on it, he falls back in line, ever eager to please, but his eyes gloss over when I try to give him additional instructions on how to avoid these pitfalls.

A few weeks into *Holding*'s Off-Broadway run, I find a producer for my own solo show. Billy panics when I tell him I will no longer be attending the show regularly. I explain, much to his consternation, that I have already overstayed my welcome—that, professionally, my job is done on opening night. Before I leave, I give Billy some pointed reminders and a detailed list of recurring notes. I meet privately with the stage manager and ask her to keep him in line.

A couple of months later, I drop by to watch the show and find that things have unraveled further. Billy is pandering to the audience and straying from the through line. My biggest concern is that he does not seem to be enjoying the work anymore. His disappointment that *Holding* has not moved to a larger theatre or taken off in a big way is becoming increasingly apparent. He is losing sight of his original intent—to entertain *and* educate by sharing something meaningful with others.

A remarkable aspect of working in a prison is the absence of bullshit. Negotiating the countless roadblocks thrown in our way by the facility's authorities affords little time for game playing or duplicitousness. I embrace that attitude when I walk backstage after the show and confront Billy. As soon as he starts making excuses, I give him the Ferrisburg stare. After a beat of resistance, he confirms that he *does* feel like he is just going through the motions and is at a loss as to how to fix it. I reiterate what I have told him so many times—to take classes and auditions, that meeting other actors and solo performers will help him realize he is not alone. I impress upon him how difficult and competitive the business can be, even when you are as enormously talented as he is, and how unreasonable it is to expect overnight commercial success. Then I get philosophical, explaining that "making it big" does not guarantee genuine happiness or satisfaction with one's career and life. I broach the delicate subject of how counseling or therapy will also help, that his life was virtually stopped for fourteen years and jumping back into it, especially into *this* maddingly frustrating and competitive business, is formidable. He listens politely, assuring me that when he has time, he will look into it. We both know just how wide a chasm he needs to cross and how difficult the first step, or leap, will be. But if anyone is up for the job, it's Billy.

Billy is an exception in that he had always wanted to pursue a career in the arts, long before being locked up. As arts programs continue to be removed from school curricula, countless young artists, passionate about pursuing a profession, are deprived of the opportunity to gain experience and build self-confidence early on. However, although most of the men I teach, and most people in general, do not aspire to a life in the arts, they nonetheless have unmined talent and a deep desire to express themselves. The disappearance of arts programs causes great harm to these students as well, for an essential component of human development becomes increasingly neglected. Its absence engenders a kind of loneliness and isolation, a feeling that something is missing, which can and *does* lead to anger and resentment and, in extreme situations, trouble with the law.

I have this wild idea: a professional acting class for the formerly incarcerated who wish to continue their training after release, where they can keep accessing those parts of themselves long ignored and, in so doing, integrate themselves into the world at large. A place where men and women are not marginalized or excluded because of the mistakes they have made but are welcomed and rewarded for the work they are doing now. A place where civilian actors and returning citizens can share with each other—the former offering practical experience and technique, and the latter demonstrating a raw and unflinching honesty unparalleled in most professional acting communities. I have this idea.

++++

As *Holding* continues its Off-Broadway run, I go back to work on *I of the Storm*, a solo show I first conceived while working at Ferrisburg. Bearing constant witness to the extraordinary turnarounds and self-discoveries of the men with whom I work inspired me to create the central character, RJ Bartholomew, a man who had it all—material possessions and social status—and lost it. Poisoned by triangulating greed and guilt over wasting his creative gifts, RJ staggers blindly into a life of avarice, eventually committing a crime and serving a prison sentence. After he is released, he ends up on the street. But it is there, stripped of his possessions and ambition, that he pursues his dream, his art—spitting poems and singing songs to anyone who will listen. In the spirit of the shows that we mounted in the prison, I abandon traditional dramatic structure—switching up genres and bending the arc of the play to the whims of its hero. It is a great departure and an invigorating release. I am rewarded for breaking the traditional rules by finding enthusiastic audiences for *I of the Storm* Off-Broadway and at several regional theatres.

During the run of my show, while I am on hiatus from the Theatre Workshop, I also develop *Me, Myself, and I*, a solo/ensemble project in which, after a performance of *IOTS*, I guide students in creating their own solo mini-shows that are then woven into a full evening of theatre. I pitch the project to a professor at my alma mater who likes the idea. But as soon as the gig is confirmed, I have reservations. For decades, I have been working with inner-city youth, remanded teenagers, parolees, and inmates. I will now be whisked to the farmlands of the Midwest to engage privileged college students on a conservative campus in a provincial town. Will I be able to make a genuine connection? Will we even speak the same language?

I feel guilty about leaving the Theatre Workshop in the lurch so, as a preview (and an apology), I arrange to present *I of the Storm* at the prison before leaving for the Midwest. I have performed the show almost a hundred times, but nothing compares to the response I received by the general population of Ferrisburg.

...treading water
try'na float
ropes get tauter
got no boat
no survivors
divers
lost
tossed
in the deep
far from the keep
a miserable heap

with voices that taunt

and memories that haunt:

"Your problem is you'll never amount..."

Don't say that I do count...

"You couldn't do it even if..."

But I want to make a diff...

Not only do the men dig the genre-bending aspect of the piece, they love the down-and-out hero and identify with his plight in a deeply emotional and *very* vocal way—hooting, hollering, shouts, wails. At one point in the Q & A, an inmate stands and calls out: "That's my life! That's *me*! Poetry and pain rubbing right up against each other!"

The talkback lasts almost as long as the show. When an inmate, Kev, asks where I will be performing the show next and I name the town in Michigan, he says his folks live a couple of hours away in Kalamazoo, and he is going to tell them to drive up and see it. His enthusiastic, best-of-intentions gesture is touching, and I admire his willingness to put the word out from the impossible place where he lives. At the end of the talkback, I acknowledge everyone who has helped make the show possible, both inside and out. Then I look out over the sea of men in green and, once again, like with the lost kitten in East New York and no regard to how I'll swing it, announce:

"As soon as I get back and get things settled, the Theatre Workshop will be starting up again. I hope to see some new faces."

A week and a half after performing *I of the Storm* at Ferrisburg in a beaten-up gymnasium under construction floodlights and a backdrop of folded lunch tables, we restage it in a state-of-the-art theatre with hundreds of modern lighting instruments and a forty-foot cyclorama. The production values are so high I wonder if the show can live up to them. And there is also the eerie business of battling the ghosts of Christmas Past, it having been forty years since I last performed on this stage. But the Ferrisburg preview gives me an anchor. The resounding endorsement by the prison population staves off any apprehension or time-warp jitters that arise. My director tells me she has never seen me so focused.

After the show I retire to the yellow, cinder-blocked dressing room (unchanged after all these years) to freshen up for the talk-back. As I head back to the stage, my director rushes down the hallway and tells me there are some people that she wants me to meet before going out. She leads me to an aisle on the end of the orchestra section where a small group is waiting. A woman steps forward with tears in her eyes and tells me that her son, Kev, is in prison at Ferrisburg and that he told her and her husband and son they *had* to see the show and so they drove up from Kalamazoo. I am stunned. Not just because Kev meant what he said, and that his folks had followed through, but because of the amazing series of events that allows a family to share a live experience despite the miles and walls that separate them. We talk for a while, everyone saying nice things about the show and how glad they are that they came. Then Kev's mother takes my hand in both of hers and smiles through the tears which now flow freely:

"That theatre program you do at Ferrisburg is changing lives. I mean it, really *changing* lives."

Mine is certainly one of them.

5

SAXOPHONE MUSIC

With two productions under our belts and a new influx of actors generated by the presentations of *Holding* and *I of the Storm*, the Theatre Workshop is hopping, desks and chairs often piled high in the corners to allow for an open space anchored by the now infamous red X. Although the facility is obsessive about spit-shining the floors, the X will often last months before disappearing, feeling like our own version of the ghost lights that are superstitiously left on by theatres during the off hours, locking in the spirit until our return each week. When the X *is* removed, I replace it with several strips that are taped to the cover of the plastic binder that holds my class material. The first time I showed up with a whole roll of spike tape it was confiscated as a weapon. The correctional officer mimed wrapping tape around his wrists: "Handcuffs."

However, I have never been questioned about the multiple strips of spike tape that I have adhered in plain sight to my binder. Noticing my stratagem, Hector remarks, "You're starting to think like us, Rich."

I have always been able to find a role for someone in a workshop production regardless of the obstacle—language barrier, learning disability, acute shyness, or hyperactivity. I have also never had to dismiss someone from the group. When the bar is raised higher than a member is ready or willing to reach, they step away, knowing they can take another shot later. Sometimes practical circumstances such as a college classes, training programs, parole preparation, or self-help groups instigate a leave of absence, but when a member does return it is old home week.

Lew has all the qualities of a so-called leading man. I cast him in an upcoming production in two roles because of his physical stature and commanding presence. Three weeks before opening, I receive an intra-prison letter from Lew stating that due to midterm exams and youth advocacy training, he has to pull out. It is a tough blow, and I have a hell of a time finding a replacement. I lose two more actors before I eventually abandon the search for a stereotypical leading man and cast someone who can, despite his unconventional looks and stature, navigate the emotional territory and learn the lines as quickly as possible. Dana, tall and gangly, bearing a crooked smile and a wandering eye, delivers a bravura performance, bringing new meaning to just who and what constitutes a romantic lead.

Two years later, as the class is forming a warm-up circle, Lew walks back into the Friday-night workshop with his tail dignifiedly tucked between his legs. His reenlistment is negotiated wordlessly, like a silent line in the Hello exercise. A simple nod from me assures him he can take his place and pick up where he left off. Lew tells the story of his workshop departure and reentry over and over at talkbacks and whenever he is interviewed about our work together. He was confounded by the lack of fanfare or remonstration when he returned—that he was merely folded back into the group. I suspect it may have been one of the few times he was given a second chance. At the postmortem of a later show in which he plays a key role, he thanks me yet again. Then he rubs his hand over the dark skin of his forearm and says:

"You're the first person I ever really trusted before that didn't have *this*."

I sometimes underestimate the impact of racial polarization in the lives of these men. I get so caught up in the work that I lose sight of how much race has affected their lives and how suspicious the men are of light-skinned folks. To many of the black and Latino men incarcerated at Ferrisburg, I am an anomaly. They are not accustomed to people like me looking them in the eye and making promises that are kept. They have a hard time believing they are really being taken seriously, conditioned as they are by a lifetime of otherness. I have never heard anyone put it as succinctly as Lew: *You're the first person I ever really trusted before that didn't have* this. His bald statement serves as a foundation for meaningful dialogue about the intense disparity of race everywhere.

++++

EMIL
So how was your day?

HECTOR
How was my day. How the fuck do you think? Shit. There's no heart out there, Emil. No heart, no soul, no jobs, no nothin'. Nobody listens, nobody fuckin' cares.

EMIL

You told them about your army training?

HECTOR

My army training I can stick right up my culo. Hey, but don't sweat it, baby. The cream always goes to the top...

EMIL

What are you doin'?

HECTOR

I'm taking five bucks, man.

EMIL

I'm handling the money, Hector. Remember? You promised.

HECTOR

I ain't ate all day!

A staged reading of Bill Bozzone's *Saxophone Music*, the story of two ne'er-do-wells co-depending their way through life, is our next project. After *Inside Out*, I know it will be some time before we are able to mount another full production and sense the men need something to aim at, a smaller project to whet their appetite. *Saxophone Music* is a modern-day *Of Mice and Men* in which Hector and Emil, who meet and become friends at a mental health facility, share an apartment upon their discharge. Hector is tough and street-smart but unable to find a foothold in life, and Emil, though mentally challenged, supports himself and his roommate by busking in the subway with his saxophone. The men in the workshop connected with the plight of the characters and the tenuous nature of their friendship.

For the role of Hector I have a new guy, Wolf. Barely five feet tall and sitting on a powder keg of repressed anger, Wolf is perfect, though I'm concerned he might resent being cast as the "angry little guy" stereotype. But, of course, that is exactly *why* I cast him—because he understands the woe-is-me, put-upon nature of the character and can imbue Hector with that quality organically. Another risky venture is Clay as Emil. Although Clay is anything but learning-disabled, he displays an emotional delay and embarrassing immaturity in class. I hope he might tap into this unawares. But what if he *is* aware? What if both men feel I am exploiting their personal characteristics for the purposes of a play?

I often wonder about tiptoeing along this line—psychological typecasting. I decided long ago that if someone ever called me on it, I would give them a proper out, but no one ever has. Casting someone as a character with parallel faults really pays off, especially when the actors see how their alleged drawbacks become strengths onstage. It makes them eager to explore and expand—to turn their base metal into gold. In a subtle acknowledgment of being cast as Hector, Wolf shares that he had been chosen in another facility to play a lion cub filled with rage in a staging of a fable by Aesop: "Guess I got issues."

The first time I ever took this kind of risk was back in summer stock, when I was directing a production of *Tom Sawyer* at a repertory theatre. During auditions I noticed a kid who stood out merely because he *didn't* stand out. Unattended by pushy parents, Mark sat quietly by himself and waited patiently. He was tall and overweight and what could most kindly be described as ... sensitive. In harsher terms,

Mark might be considered a sissy, a target for the cool crowd. When I mentally checked him off as a noncandidate for Tom or Huck, I felt guilty. After all, *I* was once that shy, sissified kid who was sidelined and excluded in the same way.

My stage manager came over, brandishing her clipboard: "We need an Alfred. I don't see one, do you?"

It was then I realized there *was* a role for this kid. Alfred was Becky Thatcher's foppish cousin, a character who was taunted and teased for probably some of the same reasons as Mark. I stalled. Was my zeal to have the perfect cast occluding my sensitivity to another human being? Was this fighting fire with fire or playing with matches? I kept going back and forth about it until I let Mark read for the part and he turned every head in the room. He proved a fine actor with great instincts and a strong stage presence, and any doubts I originally had vanished as I watched how enthusiastically the other kids responded to his work. He created an authentic, funny, and flawed character, and when we laughed, it was not at him, but at ourselves. Mark embraced the essence of who he was, bolstering his self-esteem and making Alfred a more realized character for anyone who saw him in the role.

This nervous-making tradition of hyper-typecasting works wonders. Tough guys play badasses and find their vulnerability, shy kids play wallflowers and build confidence in themselves, class clowns push it to the limit and learn restraint. Once things are set in motion, once the step is taken to accent a personality trait or limitation (or defy one), these transformations happen on their own, through discoveries that the actor makes. And anyone in the audience with similar issues is sobered and inspired by witnessing the transformation.

It certainly pays off with *Saxophone Music*. Everyone identifies with Wolf, seeing how he masks Hector's fear with bravado and hides his need for friendship and support. They cheer when Clay's hidden maturity helps Emil save the day, talking Hector off a literal ledge after a particularly brutal day. I see this alchemy play out every Friday night in the workshop, showing how using one's flaws is not only invaluable onstage but empowering and life-changing offstage. What a remarkable art form, one in which weakness becomes strength and so-called handicaps give us an advantage like no other. Theatre is a discipline in which we can achieve success not by pretending to be someone else, but by including ourselves in the process of creating a character. I am regularly amazed at the honesty and talent I encounter in the Workshop. I wonder: is it the extreme circumstances of these men's lives that bring those things to the forefront, or have we all made being *ourselves* a much harder job than it is?

When Wolf is released from Ferrisburg, he calls to let me know he is "around"—in other words, looking for acting work. I am doing a workshop for the New York City Assistant Principals of English at Random House on playwriting for young people. I plan to demo scenes from classic plays to inspire the educators to generate original dramatic material, so I hire Wolf and Vanessa, a young actress whom I met at a high school writing workshop in Bushwick. Wolf's quiet intensity and occasional flashes of fury are compelling. One of the attendees corners me after the workshop:

"Where did you find *him*?"

I tell her it's a long story.

A few months later, Wolf calls to invite me to a play at the Gerald W. Lynch Theatre at John Jay College in which his daughter is performing. He is pleased that his child shares the acting bug, and he wants to show her off. It is a Christmas pageant, which takes me back to where it all began. Staging a Nativity play was the event that started my unorthodox career of doing theatre with the uninitiated.

When I was a freshman in high school, I was approached by my younger sister's third-grade teacher when she learned I was active in the Drama Club. She asked if I would be interested in directing her "rambunctious" students in the annual Christmas play. I jumped at the chance to mount my first production. At first, I kept it traditional—shepherds in bathrobes, wise men in altar boy cassocks, angels in First Holy Communion dresses fixed with glittered cardboard wings. The narration was recited by the class's top reader and traditional Christmas carols were played on an old upright piano by the narrator's aunt. Then I got creative, introducing a red Radio Flyer wagon in lieu of a donkey, a menagerie of stuffed animals attending the manger, and a Raggedy Andy doll as the star attraction.

"Rambunctious" turned out to be an understatement. The kids were all over the place and I had no experience directing, much less harnessing their mad energy. I managed to quell the chaos when I realized that I could channel their exuberance into the show by letting them play games and improvise first. Once they felt at home onstage, they started policing themselves and things became manageable. It all went quite well until the day of the performance, when one of the angels showed up in a blue bridesmaid's dress, the white communion dress having been lost by the dry cleaners. I was convinced the show was ruined, that my *career* was over, and that I would undoubtedly be laughed out of the basement of Holy Family School.

I was completely unprepared for the kind, gray-haired woman who came up to me after the show to set me straight, telling me through a misty smile that she loved the play and thought the angel in the blue dress a stroke of genius: "An intentional flaw that showed, even with our imperfections, how cherished we are by the Almighty."

She shook my hand and told me what a bright future awaited me if I was already taking such bold risks. Then she walked away in rapture as I stood there, bewildered, my hand hanging in the air.

When I think back over the last ten years of mounting productions in a medium-security prison and all the things that have not gone right or ended up just plain wrong, the list is endless: hip radios blasting through tender moments in the show, head counts being called in the middle of tech rehearsal, script and blocking changes demanded by DOCCS that alter key moments, a broken winch causing a basketball backboard to block part of the stage, gym lights malfunctioning and remaining locked on throughout the entire performance, negating the effects of the stage lighting. But through it all, the mishaps and intentional restrictions and wrenches thrown in the works, laughter and tears have abounded in the house and the audiences have left having had a real theatre experience, undiminished by all the things that went wrong.

I am still learning that, when working under harsh conditions, with challenging populations and unpredictable outcomes, wrong is sometimes right, and bad sometimes good. That going with what is there and who I have is far more important than some idea of what or who should be there. That it is okay to shine a light on perceived flaws, including my own, to transform those flaws into beauty and humor and pathos. That great art does not need to be meticulously sequenced and planned. It can take the hits and survive upheaval. If the intent is pure, the message is strong, and the actors are real, a play will succeed not just for its artistic and technical merits, but because it fosters goodwill toward all.

6

SHOWDOWN

The Great International Scene Showcase. The title is grand, but the scenes I have accrued over the years continue to provide first-class material for my students and honor playwrights I have long admired. It also gives a boost to new actors when they realize they are working on classics—standing on the shoulders of giants, as it were. Plays like *Death of a Salesman*, *Fences*, *A Raisin in the Sun*, *The Glass Menagerie*, *Waiting for Lefty*, and *Waiting for Godot* are thrilling in themselves, but when the workshop actors encounter these masterpieces for the first time—as is, undiminished by imitation or intimidation—it is theatre at its finest.

Sometimes the men are unable to identify with the historical aspects of the plays. Analogous improvisations provide an opportunity for them to use their own lingo and play out more familiar conflicts to better understand the conditions of the dated or exotic scene on which they are working. Rather than imagine what it is like to be a suicidal Vietnam War draftee in David Rabe's *Streamers*, they tap into their own experience of being imprisoned for a crime either they did not commit or for which they are being excessively punished. Instead of trying to recreate the Great Depression and its world of small crime bosses in Odets's *Paradise Lost,* they improvise scenes illustrating the endemic poverty and gang warfare in their own neighborhoods. After playing out a closer-to-home version of the scene, they return to the original material, which is now more grounded regardless of its origin in the 1930s or '60s or '70s. The scene plays in a more contemporary way and the material comes off fresh and street, not at all passé.

When someone is baffled by dated language…

"Yo, Rich, what the hell is a *palooka?*"

… no analogy is needed, just a simple translation:

"A palooka is a bust-out asshole."

"Copy."

For the next show I cut out the middleman and write a bank of twelve original scenes based on storylines and conflicts from *The Great International Scene Showcase.* "Let's Bounce," based on *Waiting for Godot,* has two homeless men wanting to quit a shelter in Queens for one in Brooklyn while waiting on a street corner for a ride from Omar, a shady friend who never shows. "Later, Boyfriend" mirrors the Joe and Edna scene from *Waiting for Lefty,* where a woman threatens to leave her husband because he refuses to temporarily trade down his white collar for a blue one to support his family in a time of crisis. "Stand the Heat," based on Sam Shepard's *True West,* is set in East LA, where two brothers, one an alcoholic black-velvet painter and the other a gang member, compete for their absent mother's love. Michael V. Gazzo's *A Hatful of Rain* is evoked in "Crashing," where an out gay man in a Latino family attends to his homophobic brother's drug addiction.

I add two specialty pieces to bookend the show in which I appear as RJ, the director. The opener, "The Lost Sheep," starts under house lights while I'm setting up the stage furniture. One of the actors enters.

FABIR
Yo, I can't do this.

RJ
What do you mean?

FABIR
The scene. The show.

RJ
Fabir, you got this.

FABIR
No, I don't. Not with people there I don't.

RJ
You did great in rehearsal.

FABIR
Where I knew everybody. There's mad people comin' to this thing.

RJ
Welcome to the theatre. If you're so nervous why did you sign up for this to begin with?

FABIR

She made me do it.

RJ

Who made you?

FABIR

My counselor or whatever. Said she thought it would be good for me... wit' my attitude. *(beat)* Yeah, well fuck that shit!

RJ

I'm think I'm beginning to understand...

As the house lights fade and the stage lights come up full, a tug-of-war ensues as I plead with him to do the scene *while we are doing the scene.* Fabir is one of the fiercest and most physically imposing members of the cast, and so it is especially effective that he is the one who gets cold feet. Echoes of his early days in workshop, when he was resistant to (and fearful of) the work, play out in the scene as he voices his doubts about exposing himself to an audience. His confession one Friday evening was what brought the whole scene about:

"Rich, I ain't never done nothing like this before. I'm buggin'. I don't even know why I'm here."

As the character in "The Lost Sheep," Fabir explains that the upcoming performance evokes a disastrous childhood experience where he played a shepherd in a Christmas pageant and forgot his one and only line. As RJ, I share with him an experience I had in high school where I forgot *all* my lines and stood frozen in front of a full auditorium as my mother slid down in her seat. I tell him how I swore

I would never do theatre again, but in surviving the humiliation and embarrassment of that moment I found something else, a courage and tenacity that has sustained me. It registers: *that's* what he's looking for. Fabir slowly lets down his guard, his outsides no longer masking his insides, and shows us the scared little kid in our midst. It is the perfect antidote to his stage fright, and he agrees not to quit—just as the actual scene is ending.

Following "The Lost Sheep" are a dozen terse domestic conflicts stoked by economic pressures and quality-of-life challenges. Throughout the evening, attempts at reconciliation are hampered by resistance on both sides—the need to be right, the fear of change, being more comfortable with the misery one knows than an unknown and possibly better future. In each scene, one of the characters reaches a crucial point and either strikes out in a new direction or collapses in defeat. We call the evening *Showdown*.

Five of the scenes are written with female characters, so I arrange to bring in two women to play the wives, girlfriends, sisters, and daughters of the men. Once my proposal is approved by the prison, I approach Vanessa Tlachi as well as Naja Selby-Morton, another young actress with whom I worked at Random House. I know they will both fold in nicely with the show and its special circumstances. The women are enthusiastic, and once the vetting process at the prison is complete and they are cleared, we begin.

Rehearsing the male-female scenes is a dual process. I work with the women in a midtown Manhattan studio, with another actor standing in for the inmates. At Ferrisburg, several men volunteer to play the women's roles until their female partners arrive. The outside rehearsals go well, but the prison rehearsals, where the men are subbing for the women, exceed my expectations. Any apprehension I may have had about things getting campy or awkward is immediately dispelled. The men take on the women's roles as seriously as their own and turn in beautiful work. They are not the least bit self-conscious about taking a woman's point of view when dealing with the intimate workings of a difficult relationship. They revel in the roles of the wives or girlfriends whose lives *they* made difficult. It seems to be a kind of exorcism.

> I'm not playin'! I got three kids to look out for. I don't want them to hate their childhood like I hated mine. I don't want them livin' with relatives that don't want them there. And I wanna be able to hold up my head when I walk into the place I call home. I want someone who loves and respects me enough to shovel a little shit once in a while to make a better life. You and your associate degree... waitin' for a job to come along that ain't beneath you. You gotta get your hands dirty sometimes when things don't turn out like you want. You ain't the only poor son of a bitch out there with some half-assed college education that ain't worth nothin'. Grow up. Face facts. Be a man. Represent.

Horus tears the monologue up every time. I find myself giving notes to Naja and Vanessa informed by how their male counterparts are playing their roles.

It is all smooth sailing until Lew pulls out. And even after Dana replaces him, my casting woes are not over. I am now on the brink of losing another actor: Earl, the badass of *Showdown*, a tough guy with a spot so soft his own anger brings him to tears. Earl's MO is throwing shade to correctional officers, and his most recent encounter results in a loss of rec—no recreational activity—days before the show is to open.

I watch the whole thing go down on a smoke break during rehearsal. A guard, in a power play, barks at Earl to take off his hat just as he is removing it. Earl rolls his eyes and mumbles not-so-under his breath as he walks away. I pull him inside the room and tell him to let it go. But he cannot help himself, and aims his voice into the hall: "That guy is an asshole!"

I plead with him in a stage whisper: "Asshole or not, we have a show opening in a week! Isn't that more important? If you get a loss of rec, all your work will have been for nothing... and it will cause a huge problem for everyone else. It could fuck up the whole works!"

I switch gears and get lofty and inspirational about camaraderie and brotherhood, summoning the theatre gods in the hope that Earl will see the wisdom of taking the high road. He raises his voice again, knowing it will be heard by the officer in the hallway.

"That mothafuckah can't talk to me like that!"

Earl is mired in the injustice of his life, and not just the humiliation of his incarceration. He is also punching back at a lifelong sentence of not counting or being considered a part of society. None of my proselytizing about responsibility and the greater good is going to disengage him from the heat of the moment. When he is indeed hit with the loss of rec, I appeal to my staff advisor. I know advocating for Earl is a huge ask (there's no little "Inmates First" sign pinned to *her* lapel) but I speak on behalf of all the men who have worked so hard and will be adversely affected by his absence. She hears me and goes to bat for us. At the eleventh hour, by a rare show of grace, Earl is granted a reprieve.

During every rehearsal and performance of *Showdown*, I am mesmerized, watching Dana beg a friend not to forsake him for a life of

An addict and his brother reconcile in "Crashing" from *Showdown*, demonstrating a fraternal affection rarely witnessed behind the walls. **Lisa Rinzler / Courtesy of Stopped Clock Films.**

crime or Earl struggle to make amends to the pregnant girlfriend he abandoned. I am moved to tears as Pablo embraces his addict brother in forgiveness and Wood dances with the daughter that he has not seen in fourteen years. It is hard not to imagine that playing out these scenes, righting these wrongs—onstage—is going some distance toward healing painful ruptures in their own lives. And not only the actors, but the families in the audience held in the grip of the real-life drama onstage. I wonder if the settings and circumstances allow the inmates to see beyond the crimes they committed, to sense the conditioning society foisted upon them—the impossible upbringings that drove them to make poor choices and funneled them behind these walls. I hope that witnessing and experiencing these encapsulated dramas might be a first small step toward forgiving an unforgiving world, and themselves. Van's mother speaks with a tremble in her throat during the talkback:

"It's a piece of everybody's life. Everything that you said, everything that you did was part of our everyday lives.... We're all in this together."

I could not ask for a more satisfying response to a piece of theatre. One of the guests tells the men how proud they should be of themselves, and another says they evoked so many feelings and thoughts during the evening that, as a human being, he is better off for having been there. Watching the men receive this praise and gratitude is edifying. I think it is why I love theatre so much, no matter where I do it. In an allegedly make-believe world, we reach each other in ways we often cannot in everyday life—we *make believe* enough to effect real change.

++++

An "out-count" is a special arrangement where men do not have to return to their living units to be reckoned, which typically happens four times a day. I am successful in negotiating an out-count during tech and performance so the men can be available for rehearsing and for receiving notes all day and evening long. It turns out to be one of the greatest reprieves the men have enjoyed in years. Instead of banging around their housing units or working mundane jobs for pennies, they can be productive with minimal supervision. I watch my actors positioned in small groups around the gym, running lines and blocking, engaging in passionate conversations about the play, or just relaxing over a cup of coffee. Freedom pervades the room. It all seems so normal. They are just actors doing what actors do during production week in any theatre, anywhere.

The arduous process of bringing in the women turns out to be worth every painstaking step. The initial meet-and-greet is delicate, like awkward and overly polite teenagers partnering at their first dance. As things coalesce, the women fill in gaps and open emotional spaces never before explored in the workshop.

The ease with which the men and women work together is so natural that it gives a staff member concern. He stops rehearsal one afternoon to conduct a "formal orientation" for the volunteers. When I explain that I have already had one, he snaps, "Then it's time for another."

What follows is a deeply unsettling, at times harrowing, barrage of warnings about the men and allusions to their crimes. At one point, exasperated by the grave silence that greets him, he drops his clipboard and scoffs: "These are *really bad men* who have done *really bad things*."

Criminal records are irrelevant to me. I was disturbed when a friend, after attending a prison production, went home and searched the internet for the details of the actors' felonies. To witness the best these men had to offer and then sully it by digging up the worst days of their lives makes no sense to me. Sensationalism and morbid curiosity distract from our work. Preoccupation with statistics, demographics, and classifications stymies progress. Being unable to identify with and forgive the mistakes of others damages us all.

I am not interested in what my actors have done, only in who they are—now. I am interested in the remarkable effect that the arts, specifically theatre, has on those whom many consider irredeemable. I am interested in the life lessons inculcated in theatre exercises and rehearsals and performances. I am interested in seeing the best where many are unaccustomed to looking. I am interested in the courage and dignity of those unrecognized artists who unlock their secrets and risk it all, who step out onstage and show us who *we* are.

I have long embraced David Rothenberg's assertion that incarcerated men and women are *not* the crimes they have committed. The staff member who is now denigrating the men does not agree. He is particularly incensed about an incident in rehearsal that occurred that morning. Naja had broken down while rehearsing a difficult scene and two of the men had approached her afterward, offering their prison-issued handkerchiefs. At the end of his orientation he explodes: "You are NOT to take ANYTHING from the inmates!"

I am not naïve. I know the rules. I know not to accept gifts or letters or objects or written communications from an inmate. I know there are inherent dangers in those kinds of transmissions. But it saddens me that a genuinely kind and human gesture was condemned as wrong and untoward.

Not only do the women provide a broader palette of human interactions in the play, but as outside artists they validate the quality of the men's work. Naja says it is the most profound theatre experience of her career and Vanessa is in constant awe of the professionalism the men demonstrate. In the van, after our closing performance, Naja and I recount some of the highlights of the production. We laugh and shake our heads in relief, coming down from the show as theatre folk often do, totally forgetting where we are. The driver slows to allow some of the men who attended the performance to cross the road on their way back to their units. Naja and I stop talking and watch the men trudge up the hill, some still holding their theatre programs and talking animatedly.

Naja taps my arm and nods toward Vanessa, who has been uncharacteristically quiet since we left the gymnasium. Vanessa is leaning against the window of the van gazing back at the building where we worked and played for the past three days, tears silently coursing down her cheeks. During the talkback she was effusive in her praise of the men and received an ovation from her castmates after her testimony: "Coming here and being with all the guys… it's like you're all my brothers, like we're all in this together whether we're in here or out there…. It's like, you know, a powerful unity."

Naja's experience transcends artistic achievement—it is deeply personal. In one of her scenes, her character's brother is killed due to the carelessness of his best friend. The bitterness and despair she exudes is frighteningly intense at times. It isn't until afterward that I learn that Naja lost her brother in a car accident in which his best friend was driving; every night, she relived the pain of that very real tragedy. Many of the men who lost loved ones to violence and accidents have been moved by Naja's honest and unflinching portrayal of those who are left behind.

Another scene that mirrors reality for Naja is "The Step," in which she plays a young girl who confronts her father (played by Wood) after a fourteen-year separation due to his incarceration—something of which she was unaware. At the top of the scene, she is resentful and hostile toward her father's attempt at reconciliation, but when she learns the real reason for his absence, she thaws. In the final moment she tentatively accepts his apology, and then his offer to step out an old dance he taught her as a child.

When I submit the script to the prison authorities for vetting, there are two objections: a hug between Vanessa and Earl and the

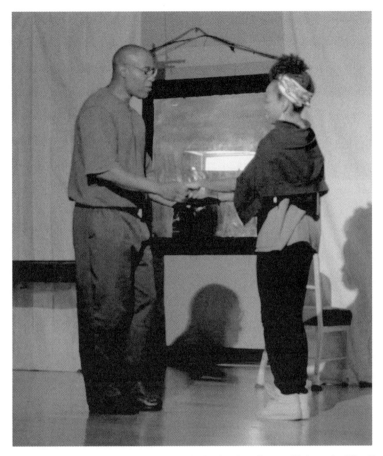

A formerly incarcerated father is reunited with his daughter for an old dance in "The Step" from *Showdown*. The prison audience wept openly as the scene played out. **Nira Burstein / Courtesy of Stopped Clock Films.**

dance with Wood and Naja, as prison protocols don't permit Wood to touch Naja's waist, or she his shoulder. I cut the hug, but have a hard time letting go of the traditional father-daughter dance. Then I remember how I taught my younger sister to dance the box step. I had taken her hands in mine and stepped it out so she could watch my feet. I make the same adjustment with my actors and, in the end, it is far more effective than the original dance. As the music begins and Naja takes Wood's hands, time stops, then rushes backward, and she appears to be his little girl once again. As they dance in the fading light to an old Luther Vandross song, the inmates in the audience crumble.

The videographer keeps the camera running during the talkbacks after performances. The men are sincere and articulate as they field questions and share their thoughts and feelings. As the microphone is passed around the gratitude pours out them:

"To do something that someone will feel proud of me."

"We try to recreate ourselves when we come within this process."

"The plus is that people actually got to see us."

"Working together, how to listen, be accountable, responsible."

"This interdependence, this bond that we have and that we share through this experience is unlike any other."

"I'm tired of keeping everything in, it's time to express myself."

"I just want to change my life, be able to say I accomplished something. Knock down that wall I built around myself."

"This has given me the will to do the right thing this time, and fly straight. This has made me so, so, so, so grateful."

The last scene in the show, like the first, is built around a conceit. As I walk out (as RJ) to thank the audience for coming, one of the actors who did not get to perform due to the loss of his scene partner (which has happened twice!) approaches me. He is indignant and resentful, demanding that he be allowed to perform before the show is over. It is another scene about not doing a scene while doing a scene, which then turns into a monologue about not having a monologue. In the climax, Gabriel, who plays the hard-done-by actor, dispatches one of the most vehement performances of the night, tapping into what the work means to him, and summing up the mission of the Theatre Workshop:

> You know... before I started doing this acting stuff I was afraid to get up in front of people because I was scared of what they would think—especially if I screwed up... and now I don't care 'cause I know it ain't about that. When I'm acting I can say things I'm afraid to say in real life 'cause I won't get in trouble if I lose it or cry or get mad or go off on somebody.... And you know what? That shit is official because when I show my emotions and stuff, when I get as real as I can get, people don't trash me or talk shit—they clap and laugh and tell me I'm good at this stuff. And... ain't nobody ever told me I was good at nothin' before. Not in real life.

At postmortems, I sometimes read an original piece as a catalyst for the sharing that follows. We have traversed the emotional globe in *Showdown*, negotiating thorny territory and uncovering long-buried feelings. The outcomes vary as greatly as the characters that are portrayed. In some, conflicts are resolved; in others, there is only the potential of healing; and several scenes end with relationships irrevocably torn by injustice and tragedy. It is the saddest of these possibilities that prompts me to share an essay I wrote about the fate of my student, Kendrick, the young man who performed *Godot* so brilliantly, and was killed by a gang member.

85

Earlier, when I read the piece at an assemblage of New York City High School teachers, it was met with weeping and rage. I expected the tears, as many teachers had lost students to gang violence, but I was unprepared for the rage. I later learned it was a bitter response to my intimation that everyone—parents, teachers, administrators, mental health professionals, politicians, and countless others—is accountable for letting kids like Kendrick slip through the cracks, for misreading or ignoring the pain behind the attitudes and rebellious behavior, for being unwilling to take a few hits instead of merely hitting back.

I sense the men will understand this better than anyone, many having had childhoods like Kendrick's. But I suspect I am also looking for an answer to a question that still throbs in my memory, a question I do not even know how to ask: *Why? Why all of this?* I know I will get emotional while sharing the piece, but I trust I can show them that. It is, after all, what I am constantly asking of them. The men are keenly attentive, many numbed and saddened as they undoubtedly recall the brothers and cousins and friends who met similar ends.

When I finish, it is quiet. Then Fabir speaks up:

"What about me?"

Before I can answer, he continues:

"I'm the guy that killed that kid."

The room goes silent. Eyes are either cast downward or fixed directly on me. I know what he means, that he did not literally kill Kendrick, but it is now abundantly clear that he killed *someone*. The antihero has spoken. The antihero who broke down in front of the audience during a talkback and told everyone how his wife died weeks before the show, and how much he regretted that she never got to see him in the play. The antihero who walked into the workshop six months before with a long, ragged beard, a homemade kufi, and a wild look in his eyes, defiant and suspicious, trying to shock me with his talk of "gangstas, macks, killas, and big willies." The antihero who switched gears when I was unimpressed by his bad-assery and tried to get my attention by throttling the exercises and scene work—and how it worked. The antihero who I eventually chose for the opening scene because if anyone knew how to set the bar in *Showdown,* it was Fabir, the little boy who forgot his line—and in a rash and tragic moment—forgot his humanity as well.

As he waits for my answer, thoughts race dizzily around in my head. What *about* him? Will the time he serves in prison really make up for the consequences of his crime? Can he ever right that wrong? Can he ever be forgiven for what he did? Can he ever forgive himself? And then an unconsidered thought arises: Or has that already started to happen?

It is natural to sympathize with victims, but much more difficult to extend that sympathy to perpetrators—the men who fill this room and the scores of other rooms and buildings around us, and around the state and the country and the world. We rarely think about the desensitization that must have taken place for people to do the terrible things they do. And yet, how is it that *these* men, sitting here in this circle, can resensitize? How is it they can show such compassion and honor and responsibility in rehearsal and performance? How is it they can embody such dignity and generosity of spirit in response to peers and audience members? How is it that they can care so deeply about this work and each other?

Does art help them do that? Does theatre? Acting? Does it give them a foothold? Does it stimulate a part of their psyche or soul that has been neglected or damaged? Does it restore an awareness of their basic goodness? I believe it does. Because I have seen it firsthand in every class, every rehearsal, every production, every talkback, every postmortem.

What about me?

We all take a bold step on a new and untraveled road tonight, with a lost sheep as our guide.

7

THIS IS THIS

I walk into workshop one Friday evening and a new guy is standing by the window, watching two groundhogs wrestle outside on the lawn. When I greet him, he turns around and smiles self-consciously, revealing a chipped eyetooth in need of repair. I ask if he is here for the acting class, as there are often mix-ups with the public speaking class across the hall. He shrugs: "Here to check it out."

Tyrique is young, and he's so quiet and diffident that I wonder what attracted him to the Theatre Workshop in the first place. Though guarded and hesitant in the warm-up exercises, he never backs off or sits one out. Later, when we are working on monologues and I need a receiver—someone to whom the working actor can address his monologue—I ask Tyrique if he will receive for Horus, who is working on a speech from *Fences* in which a father lambastes his son for his pipe dreams and lack of responsibility. Horus is doing a solid job with the monologue, but I realize that, although I am listening to Horus, I am *watching* Tyrique. He listens with his whole body, processing difficult details, fighting the impulse to respond, and examining the dilemma of his very existence before our eyes. I look around to find that everyone is equally held by Tyrique. It appears we have a virtuoso in our midst.

As I begin assembling material for our new show, I look for pieces that will challenge the men, force them out of their comfort zones. That standard, along with the high quality of Tyrique's work, ups everyone's game. The show will consist of scenes and monologues from a mixture of published and original work that must receive a unanimous stamp of approval from the cast. The goal is to make the audience feel something whether they like it or not, to *rise up off that spot.*

Our rigorous standard relegates Tony Award and Pulitzer Prize winners to the reject pile and brings lesser-known and original pieces to the forefront. The men are unimpressed by famous writers or lauded dramas if they do not meet the benchmark we have set for the show. When a classic does make the grade, it is a win-win. There is very little discussion in the selection process, just a gut reaction either way. They reject the likes of Tennessee Williams, Athol Fugard, and Arthur Miller and choose material ranging from *Jesus Hopped the A Train* to *A Raisin in the Sun,* as well as two of my scenes and a series of spoken-word narratives written and performed by our resident poet, Landon, in between scenes throughout the evening.

Two of the scenes require women—women with fire, women who will punch holes through the ceiling. In *Jesus Hopped the A Train,* I choose Francesca Ferrara for Maryann, a legal defense lawyer, overworked and underappreciated and truly at the end of her tether. Francesca is a hardworking actor and teacher who also runs a catering company and cares for her aging parents. She is a maven at handling

An overworked and burnt-out legal aid lawyer goes head-to-head with her explosive client who demands a "real" lawyer in a scene from *Jesus Hopped the A Train* in *This Is This.* **Kyle Terboss / Courtesy of Stopped Clock Films.**

crises and has the training, experience, and technique to match the roar of her scene partner, whose character accuses Maryann of ineptitude and racism. At one point her client calls her a "bumbling ass Wilma Flintstone" and Francesca nails him to the wall. For Mama in the scene from *Raisin in the Sun*, I call in Azusa SheShe Dance, who—in addition to performing her one-woman show, *Houn' Dawg: The Life and Times of Big Mama Thornton*—sings in the subway as a part of the "Music Under New York" program, drawing huge crowds. SheShe's voice is a magnificent force, hammering out blues and soul unapologetically. I know she will bring that explosive power to Mama in the confrontation with her eager-to-burn-it-all-down son.

I am gratified that the two scenes I contribute to the evening hold their own. One is from *Fathers and Sons,* where Tyrique portrays a young man confronted by an absent father who has been incarcerated for over a decade and is now on early release due to a terminal illness. Sick and dying, the father seeks out his son, intent on reconciliation. Tyrique is mesmerizing in the role. His silent, fixed stare bores a hole through the actor playing his father and when he *does* speak, each word counts as he negotiates the territory between seething bitterness and a yearning for the love he never received as child. The scene happens for the first time every time, and we all sit in awe at his consummate artistry.

When I learn that Tyrique is being released in six months (on his birthday), I begin researching scholarship opportunities for actor training at HB Studio in New York City. I pull Tyrique aside and ask if he would be interested in studying professionally, adding that I could set something up when he gets out. He giggles and rolls his eyes as if I am being absurd. When he realizes that I am serious, that I think he has the stuff, his smile melts into a disbelieving pout. I press on: "Well, would you?"

He coughs and shrugs, says he needs to think about it. A week later, during a break in rehearsal, he wanders over.

"That thing? That thing you said? Yeah... I'd do that."

Several weeks before we open, I arrive at rehearsal brimming with good news. Our request to film the show has again been approved. My technical director will be coming inside, this time with *real* theatrical lighting instruments. We now have specially constructed panels to mask the backstage, and a long-needed step unit has been built to access the stage from the audience. Francesca and SheShe are blocked and ready, having rehearsed in a midtown studio with Van, an alum of the Theatre Workshop who was released earlier that year. They are delivering the searing performances I knew they would. I have a list of over sixty outside guests who are to attend the show, including several theatre professionals and a filmmaker. I look around the room. Surprised, because he is always early, I ask after Tyrique. Frank, a new member of the workshop who holds book and sets up rehearsal furniture, looks up from the master script.

"I heard he went to the Box."

I flash on a touch football game in high school when someone sucker-punched me, and I staggered around gasping for air.

"What?"

"Something about twisting his hair and a smart answer he gave the CO."

The Box. The Hole. The Shu. Solitary confinement: the ultimate punishment exacted on inmates, deemed torture by many international human rights treaties. The mere mention of it confers a shudder on anyone in its shadow. I look around at the rest of the cast. There are a few muffled gasps, some sighs of disappointment, but mainly what I see is a lot of headshaking, a lot of *that's-the-way-it-goes-around-here.*

After a sleepless night, I call the superintendent, who immediately sloughs me off to the deputy of security who I tell how essential Tyrique is to the show (he is also giving a brilliantly comedic performance in a scene from Kenneth Lonergan's *Lobby Hero*) and how losing him will punish everyone else who has done nothing wrong. As I speak, I realize the pointlessness of it all, that I am asking a system in the business of restricting people's lives to do someone a solid. I am sure there is more to the story, but what if I am indeed trying to reason with someone who sent Tyrique to the Box for how he styled his hair? Nevertheless, I barrel on, unable to accept that we are losing the heart of the show.

When the deputy tells me Tyrique will be in the Box for at least three weeks, I assure him that even if he gets out mere days before the performance, he can still pull it off, that he is an incredible talent the likes of which I have rarely seen. (Later, looking back in hindsight, I will realize I never considered the effect solitary confinement might have on him if he *did* make it back in time.) The deputy confirms my worst fear. Tyrique will be transferred to another facility immediately after finishing his time in the Box.

He is gone. And there is not a damn thing I or anyone else can do about it.

At the next rehearsal, I replace Tyrique with two different men, as no single actor can straddle the territory he commanded with such poise. It is difficult for the new actors playing catch-up and my having to redirect his scenes from scratch, but worst is the unspoken grief we all feel at losing this unique and gifted actor of whom we were all so proud. A few weeks earlier, when I had announced *This Is This* as the title of the show, it seemed so bold and intrepid. Now it strikes me as a rebuke, a don't-want-to-wake-up call, but we soldier on, forcing ourselves not to think about it.

Our trials are not over, however. Zach, one of Tyrique's former scene partners, is a no-show on the evening of our final run-through in Room 8 before loading into the gym. I ask the CO at the front desk to call his housing unit, assuming it is a matter of Zach missing movement, the brief time allowed for the men to walk from their housing units to other parts of the prison. I ask that he be issued a late pass.

A few minutes later the CO taps on the classroom window and calls me outside.

"He's not coming."

"Why not?"

"Says he's not feeling it."

"Not feeling well?"

"Not feeling *it*."

At first, I'm confused. Then I'm livid. As the CO walks back to her desk, she lobs a grenade over her shoulder:

"Nothing we can do... this isn't mandatory."

Not mandatory—a life-changing discipline that builds character, validates being, promotes mutual respect, and incites joy. Not mandatory—in an institution where everyone's next step is planned, regimented, and scrupulously monitored as they slog through one degrading and exhausting day after another. Manual labor for literal pennies, humiliating head counts, dehumanizing strip searches, harsh penalties for unknown infractions, emasculation in front of peers, treatment not unlike slaves. The Theatre Workshop and programs like it are palliative, rehabilitating, healing. They afford men an opportunity to be a part of something, to *belong* as so few have in their lives, yet they are not requisite, not *mandatory*. The irony and tragedy of it eclipse each other—punishment for doing wrong and discouragement from doing right.

Zach returns to rehearsal the following week (*sans* apology) and is present throughout tech rehearsals and the run of the show. He turns in fine performances under the twelve-inch Source Four lighting instruments that are focused indifferently on his burgeoning ego. I am never able to count on him again. Gaining trust in this process is delicate and tricky—it often takes considerable time. When it *is* gained and then lost, it's tough to walk it back.

A few months later, when Zach is released, he calls me, and we meet for lunch at a diner on Manhattan's Upper West Side. After a quick bro hug and a barrage of reentry questions and answers, I call him on what happened. To his credit, he owns it, explaining that it was prerelease jitters, and that he's truly sorry. I won't hear from him again until two years later when a lawyer contacts me on his behalf. Seems Zach has gotten in more trouble and would like a letter of support from me. The attorney says he would also like a videotape of *A Raisin in the Sun,* in which his client "starred" while at Ferrisburg. I set the record straight—Zach played a character in a *scene* from Hansberry's play—but assure him I will pull it from the master and send it along with the letter. Before emailing the link to the lawyer, I watch the scene again. Zach delivers a rich and honest performance, exposing some of his own unflattering qualities in his portrayal of a character who is deeply frustrated with the cards life has dealt him. He displays a real earnestness that lives under his swagger.

++++

As we aim to disconnect from life's greatest misfortunes, doping kids hung from cell bars just o.d.'d found postmortem, parents departed, born discarded, derailed a train, child aborted, crippling the indigent, advocating against feminists, tax dollar embezzlement, ostracizing the benevolent, lethally injected media broadcast a fable later declared innocent but no project would save him, children inherited roles of parents swept away by the system religiously stigmatized federal cases now pending, evidence of an American nightmare was unfolding.

Landon, our poet in residence, spits the trenchant opening of *This Is This*, taking us all to task for the state of the world today. **Nira Burstein / Courtesy of Stopped Clock Films.**

On opening night, Landon, captured in a mercury-vapor spotlight and a bloodred shirt, spits his trenchant opening narrative. No one other than the cast and crew is aware of the tumult of the past few weeks. Everything runs, in the words of Clifford Odets, like "powerful motors humming in oil," and there is a buzz about the production both inside and outside the prison. The razor-sharp material pays off. As the evening's fare intensifies, the audience shifts forward on their gray metal folding chairs and become one with the cast. The climax of the show—the one-two punch of a scene from *A Raisin in the Sun* and "But for the Grace"—generates vocal "Amen"s and ardent discussion in the talkbacks that follow each performance.

A Raisin in the Sun debuted on Broadway in 1959 and, though some references are dated, the blood and sinew of the play are as relevant now as they were then, maybe more so. When SheShe marches onstage as Mama to confront her son's suspected philandering and foolish business dealings, every inmate in the audience recognizes her as his own. They have no recourse other than to jump in their seats when Mama slams a heavy metal chair down on the stage floor, and bellows, "Walter, SIT DOWN!"

It is beautiful theatre, the audience living onstage with the actors, feeling what they feel, loving who they love, cringing and crying along with the people they *know*. It is disheartening how few classic plays depict characters with which these men—mostly men of color—can identify. Witnessing the salve that a scene like *Raisin* provides for the men demonstrates unmistakable proof that there *are* solutions, ways to heal and enlighten the deprived, to put things right, to set a place for everyone at the table.

"But for the Grace," reworked from its earlier presentation in *Inside Out,* is the final scene, in which a man visits the inmate who killed his daughter while driving drunk.

I know you hate me for what I did. What I did was horrible! Don't you think I realize that? Don't you know that every day in this place reminds of that? Every day. Every hour of every day. Every time there's a head count or an inspection or a guard looks at me like I'm a piece of shit. Every day I walk on that beat-up road to work or the mess hall or back to my cell. Every time I look at the same dirt stain on the ceiling above my bed I think about it.... I was young and stupid and high on all kinds of stuff. I don't even remember getting in the car, I don't remember seeing nobody.... I don't remember anything.... I told you that. I told everyone that! I never would have ever hurt nobody if I wasn't fucked up.... I know that's not an excuse, but it's the truth! I don't know what else I can say.

An unexpected and moving act of forgiveness closes "But for the Grace" in *This Is This*, where a father's flaws make him realize that anyone can make a fatal mistake. **Kyle Terboss / Courtesy of Stopped Clock Films.**

It stuns the audience to learn that the father of the victim is not there to further reprove the inmate but to make amends, his bitterness and anger transformed into guilt and regret after his own arrest for driving drunk and injuring a young boy. The almost-ness of the event forces the father see he is no different than the inmate—that he too could have killed someone's child, that he too could be behind bars, that he too is capable of "unforgiveable" acts. Only *luck* made the difference in what they both did. At the end of the scene, the father begs forgiveness from the young man who has irrevocably changed his life—twice.

I've never realized how close to the bone "But for the Grace" cuts—until I feel the breathless silence in the house after the unexpected resolution at the end of the scene. As a coda, the characters drift back onstage echoing salient lines from their scenes and initiating a dramatic finale that lifts into song:

My momma told me honey it's gonna be a long summer
And if you get caught you're gonna see a long number
Gotta fold up the deck, gotta roll with the thunder
They ain't holding us back, they ain't holdin' us under....
And I feel what they sayin'
And I can hear 'em when they prayin'....
What we gotta do to survive, survive, survive, survive
In this cold, cold world, survive, survive, survive
In this cold, cold world.

As the anthem that Zach composed during the rehearsal process rings through the house, only the occasional bark of a hip radio or the appearance of a CO in the wings reminds me that we are not in a legitimate theatre but on the sparse platform of a gymnasium in an upstate prison.

One night, before the show, a prison official dresses Wood down in front of the entire cast and crew, berating this respected leader in the workshop as a principal would a recalcitrant child—all because he forgot the plastic spoons when setting up hospitality before the show. Wood stands in the corner with his head bowed and takes it. We are all embarrassed by the scene, and each of us tries to covertly reassure him afterward. Wood rolls his eyes—*no big deal*—but it is obvious he is diminished by the scolding. It seems to have an even greater consequence at the final performance.

During the opening scene on the last night, when we are filming, a large summer fly makes its way into the gym. I know it will be a challenge to the actors and I hope everyone will just let it be. Still shaken from the censure, Wood releases some of his pent-up anger and takes a swat at the fly. It disappears instantly—and so do his lines.

I see a look in his eyes that I know all too well as an actor—when you run short on rehearsal time, when a playwright edits the script right up until opening night, or when unforeseen distractions like cell phones and banging pipes invade the sanctity of the theatre. More times than I care to admit I have "gone up"—lost my lines—and wanted to die. Through the years I have shared these experiences with my actors, explaining how I learned to keep talking no matter what, to breathe, to trust your partner, to know that your sense of the play or scene or monologue will ultimately win out. On the closing night of *This Is This*, I see the passing on of that harried tradition. What comes out of Wood's mouth in no way resembles what is written but, lines be damned, he goes on, making as much sense as he can until the earth shifts back on its axis and he finds solid ground.

At the postmortem the following evening, Wood is once again at the center of a shitstorm. Seated in a circle, sipping instant coffee, we go around the room as usual, each man sharing their experience of the show. It's business as usual until Frank describes how his friends razzed him for missing basketball practice to rehearse for his "stupid show." He snorts, forgetting he's not hanging with his homies, and drops the bomb:

"Those n———s are crazy, yo!"

Wood shoots out of his chair and launches into a monologue far more turgid than the one he delivered in the show even when he *knew* his lines. Although the camps are divided by age as to the inappropriateness of the N-word and the difference between using a "hard R" or not, Wood is on fire:

"After *all the shit* we been through, showin' people what we *can* do if we set our minds to it, you gonna put us back in the same damn hole we been in our whole fuckin' lives?!"

Wood storms out into the hallway while Frank tries, unsuccessfully, to laugh it off. My head is spinning. This is not the first time I have been at this deadly intersection. During *Showdown,* I allowed the use of the N-word in a scene in which a young mother, in anger and frustration, confronts the deadbeat father of her child and lambastes him with the hateful invective. I had heard the "R"-less pronunciation of the word used in conversation around the room during rehearsals, and I naïvely thought it acceptable to use onstage. When several of the older men objected vehemently, it was excised, but we never talked about it. I did not condone *or* condemn it—didn't ask nor tell. I convinced myself that it was not my place to make pronouncements on these things, that I did not understand the complexities of how this word affected people of color. After Wood's explosion, after seeing his look of deep disappointment and shame, I knew I could no longer justify my non-committal attitude. My rationalizations were bullshit. When is it *not* your place to speak up and say what you feel?

Opening an old wound, I take the floor and explain what happened during *Showdown.* This time, I go on to say what I did not say then: That I was wrong. That after all the years of working in the prison, I could *feel* the word in the air, a miasma, oozing from inside and outside the walls. I can see how racism has shattered our nation and that mass incarceration is not just a liberal buzzword but a brutal and tragic fact of life—and that the N-word is often the instrument of that hatred and fear and injustice. It was wrong in *Showdown,* and it is wrong at any time, in any case, with any spelling or pronunciation. There is no reason or excuse for using one of the most destructive and hateful words created by humankind. My coffee cup trembles in my hand as I tell them I made a mistake, a *big* mistake.

That night I go home and write a preamble for the workshop. I read it aloud before starting our next class. I have read it ever since whenever I begin with a new crop of actors:

The Theatre Workshop is a safe room. During exercises and improvisations, it is hoped that all feel free to speak honestly and openly. The only language that will not be tolerated is language that demeans or stigmatizes others—words that promulgate racism, misogyny, homophobia, transphobia, or any slurs regarding appearance, culture, or disability. The purpose of art, in this case theatre, is to develop our higher selves, to connect with our fellows, and to illuminate the human condition with love and respect.

"Do not fear mistakes. There are none." I often quote Miles Davis, driving home the idea (often to myself) that what most of us call mistakes are probably the most important and transformative moments of our lives if indeed we, or others, learn from them. I know that exposing your missteps to your students terrifies a lot of teachers, but I've found it is the only way I can connect with them authentically. I have to let down my guard, be merely another actor, another person, as terrified as they are. After all, I don't have the answers, just some experience I can pass along.

Mistakes are an integral, necessary part of theatre work—we need them to portray the flawed, beautiful characters that people the stage. We need the mess and the gaffes and the train wrecks so we can broker the thorny conflicts and complex relationships we must confront. Rehearsing for a show often feels like practicing for life—deliberately putting on the pressure to see how we will hold up, how we will *act*. If we are enough.

Despite the lines we forget, the money that falls through, the gate-keepers who bar the way, the authorities who put us down, the heroes who don't show, the history that threatens our work, the colleagues we lose, the talent that is wasted, and the *flies* that madden us into panic, leaving us vulnerable and unsure of what to say or do, what matters is that we keep doing it. We walk to the center of the room. We look in each other's eyes. We play our parts as sincerely and truthfully as we can.

8

FATHERS AND SONS

On a Friday evening in late April, I notice an oak-tag poster taped to the wall of the anteroom in the arsenal announcing an upcoming Mother's Day celebration at Ferrisburg—a musical tribute, games for children, refreshments. It is one of the most altruistic events I have ever seen promoted at the prison. The Volunteer Recognition Dinners, Talent Shows, annual religious and education ceremonies, and Theatre Workshop productions provide a respite from the mind-numbing drudgery of prison life, but there is something about honoring the long-suffering mothers and wives of the incarcerated that I find particularly affecting. In class, I ask the men if there is a similar event for Father's Day. I am met with a roomful of icy stares.

"They don't do nothin'."

A remount of the play that started it all seems not only a good idea, but a clarion call—*Fathers and Sons*. I adapt the two-hander for a cast of fourteen, removing extraneous material, adding new scenes, and creating a finale (as is now a tradition in our shows) that will serve as a not-so-veiled tribute to Father's Day. When I aim for a June production, as close to the unrecognized holiday as possible, the men are hesitant, fearful the timing might be perceived as an affront to the administration, and so we move the dates to early July. Subterfuge notwithstanding, the men are enthusiastic about tackling the subject and honoring the day. A lot of the guys are attempting to parent their children from inside the walls, many without having had a father or male figure as a role model. We address this throughout the play, dramatizing how, without a road map or manual, fathers and sons find ways to come together, to help and love each other.

Fathers and sons. A subject that has been a constant in my writing and theatre work. I was terrified of my father until I was twenty-six, when he died of alcoholism and lung cancer, and even death did not liberate me from his tyranny. My father was an angry and violent man who tried to beat out of me the loathing he had for himself. It instilled a fear and insecurity that haunt me to this day. One of my first short stories goes at it unexpurgated:

The wooden, open-tread stairs to the cellar vibrated under the weight of the boy's father. The boy waited at the bottom, as he had been told, to have the shit kicked out of him. The untied laces of his father's work boots slapped against the side of the staircase as he strode down. The boy moved to the center of the concrete floor, the oil furnace rumbling behind him. His father removed his belt. The boy could feel the urine running down his legs and taste tears at the edge of his mouth and No, No, I'm sorry, No, No, Please... would not prevent the beating—because his father was drunk. But not too drunk. He was at that crazy halfway place when the boy knew that nothing he said or did, no amount of tears, would stop him. All the boy could do was scream inside his head and take it.

My father always told me that he was the boss of the house, he paid the bills, and as long as I lived under his roof I was to do as he said. *Don't do as I do, do as I say.* He also told me that if I ever dared to lay a hand on him it would take three cops to pull him off me. And he told me that I didn't have the brains I was born with and that I should be ashamed of myself. And he always told me to get out of his sight.

I once remarked to the men, many of whom had never known their father, that I sometimes wished I had been fatherless as well. They did not feel the same. The idea of at least *having* a father, no matter how horrific, seemed preferable to not having one at all. In my case there *were* moments of surrender, of coming together—when he was too hungover to wreak havoc, when the memory of his crippled mother brought him to tears or when, inexplicably, he would insist we play dodgeball in the dead-end street on which we lived. But these were brief windows soon shattered by a backhand to the face or a vicious and humiliating putdown in front of friends. The only real connection we had was shortly before he died, when he was too tired and weak to blow up everything around him. I remember shaving him in his hospital bed as he lay dying—holding a razor to the throat of a man who had pounded me down more times than I could count. But my revenge fantasies were dispelled by his sincere gratitude for my service, for restoring some dignity to a man who was obsessed with appearances but could never look inside. That final window soon closed forever.

I knew I had broken the generational chain of abuse when my son ran *to* me when he was frightened, by a scary Halloween costume or an angry dog or a bad dream. I had always fled from my father, as he was almost always the source of my fear. With help, I learned to be the father I never had, and it certainly went a long way in ameliorating old wounds, in forgiving a man who could not give away what he did not have.

Throughout my teaching career, I have become an unwitting father to many of the kids and grown men who were abandoned by their fathers or scarred by abuse or neglect. It is difficult to watch men who cannot (or will not) access therapy or recovery, whose wounds continue to fester as they struggle blindly through life, passing on their misery to their sons. In my work with at-risk teenagers, incarcerated men, and parolees, I see all too clearly this fatal disconnection between parents and children. Perhaps even sadder are cases where families *are* present, *are* caring and protective, yet the poverty-stricken, drug-infested, and crime-ridden neighborhoods in which they live corrode these relationships, luring many innocents away.

++++

I met Raul when he was sixteen years old and attending Drama Rep Academy, an alternative high school in midtown Manhattan. Raul had grown up in Harlem and was one of the most talented actors with whom I had ever worked. The first few weeks in class he was a joy—fearless, open, honest, willing to get up onstage and show you who he was, even as he was discovering that for himself. He was an innately gifted artist with great instincts and charisma, and I was perplexed as to why he was never involved in any of the progressive school's plays and talent shows. A teacher at the school explained to me that Raul had once highjacked a show, going off-script and pandering shamelessly to the audience. I chalked it off as an innocent mistake borne of inexperience, ignored the warning, and learned a brutal lesson over a decade later.

The first time he showed up high to a showcase, I refused to let him perform. To his credit (and as a sign of his desperation to act) he never did it again. However, as the year went on, I noticed a steady and gradual downward slide. He missed classes more and more often and his lateness was constant and infuriating, making it increasingly clear why he had been given a wide berth by the other arts professionals at the school. I suspected that the drug habit he now kept out of my classes and rehearsals was accelerating during his quickly expanding free time and negatively impacting the very thing he had been trying to protect. But Raul always managed to pull it together right before the axe fell, making impressive strides in class and turning in first-rate work. Whenever he came through at the last minute, and I saw his triumphant smile after a brilliant performance, it fed my hope for an ultimate victory of ardor over addiction.

Then he dropped out. The principal and I joined forces in trying to reenroll him at a less stringent school so that he might graduate. He showed up for the initial interview but never followed through. I later learned that if he did graduate from high school, he would have been the first in his family to do so. There seemed to be a skewed sense of loyalty that prevented Raul from standing outside the pack, from leaving those he loved behind. It made me wonder how many other dropouts feel the same way.

A series of random events kept us working together—play readings and acting demos, school shows and tech work on professional productions. But the lateness and intermittent no-shows continued and accelerated. Attributing it to a chronic substance abuse problem,

I slowly pulled away. After one too many times of Waiting for Raul, I called it quits. It would be years before he resurfaced.

When he did, I was at the Cornelia Street Café trying out the material that would eventually become *Fathers and Sons*. Greeting guests at the door, I looked up to see Raul standing there, grinning ear to ear. Not only was he clear-eyed and upbeat—he had *paid* for his ticket. He introduced me to his new girlfriend, who was lovely and articulate, quite a departure from the girls he ran with back in the day. He loved the work I shared that evening, and his sudden reappearance was too much of a coincidence to ignore. With newfound purpose, I grafted our long and shaky relationship onto a series of vignettes and created a through line for *Fathers and Sons*: an acting teacher and his protégé discovering the nature of their own father-son relationship through the volatile and affectionate scenes they played onstage; a play within a play *within* a play.

Things moved quickly. I secured a producer, a director, and a respected venue Off-Broadway on Theatre Row. Rehearsals went so well that I did not know whether art was imitating life or the other way around. Raul was prompt, reliable, and cooperative. It appeared we were writing the culminating chapter of our unique relationship. And we were—but not in the way either of us would have wanted. As the more commercial aspects of the production infiltrated the process— interviews and publicity, designers and attending staff—I watched Raul's personality slowly swell into something I did not so much recognize as remember being warned about. His occasional cockiness was now the norm: lateness crept back in, and he called in sick at the most inopportune times. He began misbehaving in rehearsal, taking issue with his notes, questioning the director (and the playwright). After we opened, he became emotionally erratic, snapping out or holding back unexpectedly. I began fearing that lines and cues would be the next to go. It was unnerving to me as his acting partner but enraging and painful as his teacher and friend. During the final week of the run the only time we spoke or looked at each other was onstage, in character.

I had not foreseen that the play, in which the protégé is fired, would imitate life as startlingly as it did or that it would trigger the abrupt ending for which neither one of us was prepared. After the curtain call for our last performance, as we walked offstage in silence, we suddenly stopped, turned to each other, embraced, and wept. After some vague muttering about calling and writing and talking, we went back to our dressing rooms, and then left the theatre separately. It would be five years before we met again.

The rewrite and staging of *Fathers and Sons* at Ferrisburg is transformative. Removing the teacher-student narrative and focusing on the father-son vignettes brings even greater clarity, illuminating the intricacies and generational obstacles that have made this relationship so impossibly difficult through the ages. When a son wants to break free, a father slaps him down. When a father begs for forgiveness, his son attacks.

Let go of this? How can I let go of this? It's who I am. It's all I know. Because of you I'm afraid all the time. I don't know how to be a father to my own son. I don't know how to DO my life because nobody was ever there to show me. And it eats away at me all the time knowing there's nothing I can do about it. That there's no way I can change the past and that I feel like I don't have a future. I've been fucked up for so long.

As Father's Day approaches, we lose two cast members, both sons. One is transferred to another facility without warning, but his understudy is in place and the work continues without a beat. The loss of the second son is much more difficult.

When Arlo first arrived in class, he watched from the corner of the room and never spoke. When he did step forward to take part in exercises, he was still watching, not really immersing himself in the work or giving over to the group. Because he was the youngest in the company, I cast him as the drug-addicted teenage son whose beleaguered father leaves him to his fate in a police precinct. It was a risky move, but I sensed Arlo had it in him, and he did—to a point. At the end of the scene, when his father abandons him, when he is supposed to break down and scream for deliverance, Arlo's throat would close, trapping his feelings inside. I tried coaxing him, using improvisatory and emotive exercises to free him up but every time he moved toward the edge he stopped before the moment of truth. One day, he confessed:

"Rich. This happened to me! This exact same thing happened to me!"

Konstantin Stanislavsky based his revolutionary system of acting on fusing a character with the actor's memory and life experience. He encouraged actors to access emotional states directly: *jump and the net will appear.* This approach does not work with Arlo. Playing a scene that he has lived through is exactly what is stifling him. Taking a terrifying risk after everything he has been through, or trusting that someone has his back, is just too fucking ridiculous for him to even consider. I sense his paralysis emanates from the fear that if he does *go there,* he might not be able to get back—especially considering the environment in which he now lives.

But Arlo surprises me, surprises us all. He begins to trust the group and to carry his own weight. He becomes an integral part of a process where everyone is pushing emotional boundaries and taking risks. It is thrilling to see him step down a road he has never dared travel. As he reaches deeper and deeper inside, it effects a physical transformation onstage. We are all stunned into silence the day he slams his fist on the table and begs his father shamelessly, his throat open, his body trembling:

> Dad, this time I mean it! I swear to God! This time I do want it, I'll do anything... I promise... Dad! Daddy! You can't... How can you do this to me? You can't leave me here! Don't you love me? Dad! Come back! I'm sorry! Please! Dad!! You can't! YOU CAN'T DO THIS TO ME!

Exposing his rage and sorrow leaves Arlo breathless and in shock. As rehearsals progress and he gets his bearings, he becomes more comfortable with being uncomfortable and no longer seems to care who sees it. It is as if, finally, he *wants* us to see it, to see him. Arlo ups the ante when it comes time for family invitations to the show. Each man is allowed four family members. Most have only one or two on the list, some have none. Arlo has all four. Then he catches a loss of rec.

A week after he is removed from the show, I see Arlo outside the gym in line for a phone call. I wave and he nods back. A little while later, breaking the rules, he walks into the gym, all smiles, to say hello to his former castmates. He takes a spin around the room and is in the middle of saying, "I really miss you guys..." when a correctional officer bursts through the gym doors and excoriates him for the impromptu visit. The officer had been listening and watching for a while and does a very bad acting job of impersonating Arlo and mocking his enthusiasm. He tells Arlo he'll soon *really miss* everyone and every<u>thing</u> if he ever pulls a stunt like this again—a not-so-veiled threat to send him to the Box.

Nothing mitigates the shock and sadness of having an actor pulled from the show at the eleventh hour. For the actor, it is the loss of a unique opportunity to walk back misdeeds and misconceptions, to do something that matters, to reconnect with the world. Arlo never gets the chance to share with an audience what he worked so hard to find. But he *did* find it. We saw it in rehearsal every Friday. In revealing who he was, he discovered who he could be.

"I said shut up!"

"No, you shut up!"

A father and son struggle to come together after the father's fourteen-year absence due to his incarceration in *Fathers and Sons*. **Nira Burstein / Courtesy of Stopped Clock Films.**

The first scene opens with bombast: an unemployed father ridicules his son's entrepreneurial efforts while the son lays bare his father's complacency and failure at self-realization. The scene closes with a backhand to the son's face that brings gasps from the audience and a lot of shuffling among the officers assigned to the gym. The next scene has two workshop veterans quietly breaking our hearts in a bilingual scene where a first-generation immigrant son, after receiving a scholarship to a prestigious university, reveals his embarrassment about his kind, loving, and illiterate father. Then we cross-fade to a corporate office where a successful business owner offers his son everything that money and power can buy, except what he needs most—his attention. After losing two young Caucasian actors in succession, I bring in my nephew to play the son after someone remarks, "You're gonna have a tough time finding another white boy around here."

The "Quartet" is at the heart of the show—two interlaced scenes that segue at key moments. A single father anguishes over placing his mentally challenged adult son in a group home, while another son tries to convince his widowed father he must move into a long-term care facility due to his advancing dementia. An actor new to the workshop renders the afflicted father so simply and honestly it gives even the most impenetrable CO on duty pause. And Royal's show-stealing portrayal of a mentally challenged son brings laughter, tears, and an innocence that disarms everyone. He later shares that his performance is a tribute to the special-needs children of one of the kinder staff members. I suspect this is what keeps his work so humble and grounded.

A controversial scene in the police station, where a father refuses to enable his son's addiction—the scene Arlo never got to play—disturbs inside and outside audiences equally. At each performance Juan, as the father, breaks down in real tears as he makes the hardest decision of his life:

> How many fuckin' times? How many rehabs and programs and meetings and counselors? I remortgaged the goddamn house to pay for all those things. And none of them did any good because you don't want it, Migue. You just don't want to stop. I can't do it no more.... I love you more than you'll ever know. That's why I can't watch you kill yourself.

The show closes with an unexpected deathbed reconciliation between a formerly incarcerated man and his son, both struggling with an inherited drinking problem. The confrontation is instigated by the son having a child of his own, and his desire to break the chain. The father/grandfather is played by Mohammed, a lifer, who held supporting roles in previous productions and now, deservedly, commands the lead. He is a stalwart member of the group, never missing a class or

A father admits his inability to parent his son because he was abandoned by *his* father as a child in *Fathers and Sons*. **Nira Burstein / Courtesy of Stopped Clock Films.**

rehearsal. He is off-book after only a few rehearsals, and he always has the coffeepot set to brew before workshop starts.

The following year, Mohammed will be released after serving over thirty years. Eight months later, he will collapse and die in the street. Moze, who asked the question that defined my work at the prison, will slip away in his sleep mere months after being released. Tragically, this is not an uncommon fate for those with long sentences, owing to decades of bad nutrition, poor health care, and unfathomable stress. I will never forget Mohammed's face in the final moment of *Fathers and Sons* as he lay on a deathbed fashioned from milk crates and blankets, smiling rapturously, having sought and received the thing he wanted most in his long and difficult life: forgiveness from his child. Once, at a talkback, in front of the inmate audience and outside guests, Mohammed broke down, expressing his remorse for the crime he committed—a rare occurrence in my many years of working at Ferrisburg. That sincere contrition reemerged every night in Mohammed's performance, enlightening and inspiring us all.

FATHER
Ed, I didn't want any of this... any of that to happen.

SON
But it did.

FATHER
I know. I used to write you letters in prison all the time trying to tell you how much I missed you growin' up... missed havin' my boy.

SON

How come you never sent any of 'em?

FATHER

I could never... get it right. But I wanna say something now, though, and I guess it don't matter no more how it sounds, only that I say it. Don't run away from your feelin's like I did. Don't let that screw up the rest of your life.

SON

You're the one who screwed up my life.

FATHER

I know I did. I messed up real bad. And believe me, if I could change that... Oh Christ, baby boy if I could.

++++

After the show, the men in the audience bolt from their seats to grab the proffered microphone and share their thoughts:

"I really didn't know what to expect.... I didn't anticipate being so touched, truly sincerely touched by everyone.... This to me was perfect... perfect in so many ways. It is something that we all need. So therapeutic, so cathartic...."

"It wrenches us... as men. We want to become better people, to become better human beings... become better fathers and sons."

"You guys all took me out of prison for a few hours and that was... amazing."

Fathers and Sons gives the men a voice—a chance to say *we are here* or, à la the Actor's Vow, *we will be heard*. There is also a perceptible thaw among the correctional officers who are assigned to the gym during production week. Some even request the posting to see the show, and others are less disruptive while the play is running. Loading the equipment in and out is smooth and hassle-free. A minor counting error in one of the inventory lists, usually cause for a major foofaraw, is dismissed out of hand, the sergeant looking up from his clipboard and saying that he *trusts* me. I am not exactly sure why this show has such an effect on everyone, but I suspect that putting front and center one of humanity's most difficult and compelling relationships tenders even the hardest hearts.

The most unexpected act of goodwill occurs on the last evening of the run during dinner break. "Nana," one of the tougher officers at Ferrisburg, is assigned to the gym for the show. Small and callous, she appears to be holding on to the job well past retirement age. The men are alternately amused and enraged by her. She reminds me of an urban version of Mammy Yokum from the *Li'l Abner* comic strips. Whenever Nana works Building 112 on Friday nights, she scrutinizes my ID as if it might be fake and asks for the umpteenth time where I am from and when I will be leaving. She often pulls men out in the middle of my class to berate them for wearing hats or neglecting to pick up their IDs on time. Our worst collision occurs when I step outside the building one evening to remind an actor, on his way to mosque, about rehearsal later that evening. She tears out of 112, rips into me on the pavement for not having an official escort and reports me to the lieutenant, who later pulls me out of 112 to finish what she started. Whenever I see

Nana sitting behind the desk on Friday evening, I know it won't go easy.

For the last performance, we receive permission to have pizza brought in for dinner. There is a misunderstanding when the pizzas are ordered and we receive several extra pies. When an announcement is made about the surplus, I notice Nana circling the stack of boxes. I grumble under my breath, "Don't even think about it."

But again, a mysterious aura of goodwill pervades, and something shifts. Despite the grief she has always given me and my actors, I un-dig my heels, walk over to her station, and extend an olive branch:

"Would you like a slice?"

She doesn't break character:

"No, no, I don't need nothin'."

I force a smile:

"Well, if you change your mind, you're welcome."

She takes two slices. From then on, I will never have an issue with her. She even comes to the rescue during that night's performance when our cameraperson's equipment malfunctions, rushing over and silently escorting the filmmaker to a side room so she can reconstitute the device, and then walking her back to the gym. The men say they have never seen anything like it. Was it the power of the play? Was it my gesture? Was it the pizza? It no longer seems important *why* it happened. Only that it did.

++++

Several months after the show, I notice a poster for a staged reading of a play being presented by a new theatre company in my neighborhood. When I see Raul's name on the flyer, I decide to go. I am unsure what I am looking for. All I know is that we never resolved the conflict, just stopped the bleeding. After the reading, I stand outside waiting, nervous about opening it all up again. Raul is genuinely surprised to see me and warm in his greeting. We hug, and then he kisses me on the cheek, something he has never done before. It harkens back to my youth when my father who, despite his violent and hurtful ways, had always greeted me with a kiss after a long separation. Raul asks if I'll join him and the cast for drinks and I go along. When he introduces me to everyone as his mentor, I jokingly refer to him as my tor-mentor and we both laugh—laughter borne of old pain.

We sit at a separate table and after a bit of catching up are silent. Raul makes a rambling apology for his behavior in *Fathers and Sons*, for which I am more grateful that I thought I would be. Then he tells me something for which I am completely unprepared.

He got in trouble a couple of years after the show, was swept up during an errant drug deal and, after accepting a plea bargain, was sent to a boot camp upstate for a little over a year. As he recounts the events of his incarceration, he scrutinizes my reaction, knowing of my prison work and what has always been his unforgiving attitude: *Bad people deserve what they get.*

But there is something else in his gaze that evening, a secret smile, an imminent confession of something he knew I would understand better than anyone else:

"I started a theatre group when I was there. And we did a show. I used a lot of the exercises you taught me.... It was awesome."

Something *had* gotten through. Not the censures and scolding and life lessons, not anything I had ever said. What got through was the thing that I loved, and that he loved. The thing we *had* to do to be who we were. And in one of the darkest and most frightening times of his life, Raul went toward the light, and it delivered him.

We have not met or spoken since. I am not sure if we ever will. But I will always be thankful for what he taught *me*. That even when I stay in there a bit too long, overzealous and needing to be useful, if my genuine intent is to pass on what was given to me, the love of what I do, that intent will find its way into the hearts of even the most difficult, who may one day, under unforeseen circumstances, retrieve it and pass it on to someone else.

9

ALL MY SONS

Some of the men are putting together parole packets and ask for a certificate that documents the work they have done in *Fathers and Sons*. The deputy of programs approves the idea and as I list their impressive accomplishments—Physical and Vocal Exercises, Deep Reflex Response Work, Theatre Games, Sense Memory Training, Script Analysis, Intermediate and Advanced Improvisation, Scene and Monologue Work, Stanislavsky Technique Training—I realize they have received what amounts to several semesters of theatre training, so I investigate the possibility of the men receiving college credit for their work through CUNY's college-in-prison program for future shows. I learn that this is indeed possible, but only for the men who are formally enrolled as CUNY students.

In the fall of 2019, I teach my first accredited class at Ferrisburg and am dubbed "Professor Rich" by both my CUNY class and the Friday-night workshop. When I submit my first syllabus for review, I wonder how the deputy will respond to the titles of such exercises as Ripple, 21, Hello, Whatever You Say, There Is No Four, Gimme, and HWAH! I also wonder if they will take exception to a Tove

Jansson quote I include that preaches not only to the choir but the whole congregation:

> A theatre is the most important sort of house in the world because that's where people are shown what they could be if they wanted, and what they'd like to be if they dared to—and what they really are.

I hope being a legit professor for a city university will eliminate some of the roadblocks I encounter on Friday night as a volunteer, that there will be more respect for a prestigious educational institution than a voluntary recreational program. Not so much. There seems to be resistance, even some resentment toward CUNY that manifests as delays in arsenal processing, missing gate passes, and thirty- to forty-five-minute waits for vans. There is also an increase in student absenteeism, as ill-considered scheduling of mail pickups and medical exams causes the men to miss an entire class because of an appointment or errand that takes minutes.

Spot inspections in the housing units are more frequent, stopping movement. Men wearing pocketed T-shirts or do-rags are turned back and miss entire classes. Sitting in their housing units while their class is being conducted down the road seems not unlike high school suspensions, where students are punished for questionable behavior by being deprived of the education that is designed to correct that very behavior.

Many of the prison staff do not have college educations and I suspect they fear these *criminals* are gaining an unfair advantage. But the biggest resentment is the astronomical tuitions many of the men and women who work in the jail are paying to put their children through college, while the CUNY students are getting what they deem a free ride. The financial struggle of the officers is certainly understandable, but I wonder if they ever consider that these men are paying dearly for an education with the most precious commodity afforded anyone: their freedom. After years of incarceration, solitary confinement, and drudgery, how can one not see the universal benefit of allowing these men an opportunity to grab hold of the first rung in a climb toward stability and dignity?

++++

"Work like crazy—think they'd see it? You'd drop dead first!"

"I don't want to be criticized—nobody takes me serious here!"

"We're still under the ice, you and me, we never escaped."

"Do you think I like this feeling of no possessions?"

"What did I want? To be a great man? Get my picture on a postage stamp?"

"You don't know what it's like to sit around here and watch the months go ticking by."

"All I want's a chance to get to first base!"

When Odets wrote those lines, I doubt he had any idea how they resonate with the incarcerated. As my students speak his words in a prison acting class, they inhabit not just the struggle of the working-class poor but the longing for a stolen childhood and the dreams on which the young thrive:

When I was a kid, I laid awake at nights and heard the sounds of trains... far-away lonesome sounds... boats going up and down the river. I used to think of all kinds of things I wanted to do. What was it? Just a bunch of noise in my head?

For the men taking courses at Ferrisburg, it is *not* just a bunch of noise in their heads. They are going to college. Their campus walls are trimmed with barbed wire instead of ivy. They do not stroll through a pine grove on their way to class; they instead lumber down a crumbling tar road. But this training—this *education*—allows them an internal freedom to make choices that urge them forward, where they can learn to accept guidance, where they can tap into resources of which they have been long unaware.

Grady has been a redoubtable pain in the ass all semester—disruptive, giddy, questioning every note he is given. His attendance is spotty and his smirk impenetrable. I give him a monologue from David Mamet's *Glengarry Glen Ross* almost as a rebuke; it's delivered by the character Richard Roma, a hedonistic smartass musing on the meaning of business and sex. Grady instinctively capitalizes on his own smugness to render the character authentic to the play, and then some.

But it is the scene from *All My Sons* that not only surprises and intrigues him but awakens something. Arthur Miller's harsh drama disarms Grady, stranding him in foreign territory. Growing up father-less, Grady often alludes to being family-less as well, having spent most of his youth in an unending series of foster homes. His early trauma was later compounded by the brain injury and PTSD he suffered during a tour in Iraq. After his discharge, he often found himself on the wrong side of the law, which eventually led to his current bid. In the scene, Grady calls out his father on a heinous crime hidden from his family for years. Playing the role of someone who is, for once, in the right empowers and consumes Grady. He takes his errant father to task, finally able to give voice to the abandonment he experienced in his own childhood and unleashing a ferocity he has withheld for decades.

On the day of the Final presentation I walk into the room with some outside guests in tow and find everyone ready and waiting—except Grady. I shake my head in defeat, fearing that despite all the hard work and his breakthrough in *All My Sons,* he is bagging it. Self-sabotage is all too familiar in this environment, a trap into which a lot of men fall completely unaware. I throw up my hands:

"Where the hell is Grady?"

One of the men looks up and smiles:

"He's over in the other classroom practicing his lines."

I walk across the hall and look through the window and indeed there he is, animatedly running blocking and lines, stopping, making corrections, and starting and stopping again. Grady could be in a rehearsal studio at Juilliard for all the focus and discipline he demonstrates. As soon as I open the door, he turns to me and grins. It was a setup—he *wanted* me to catch him in the act.

A colleague makes the trip up from the city when she learns that one of the men in my class is a student she taught at another facility. She found Shon to be an extraordinarily talented writer and is fascinated by the idea of him now studying acting. Shon is performing a monologue from *Golden Boy* in the role of Joe Bonaparte, a young boxer who is torn between fighting professionally and his real love, music. My friend is privy to the circumstances that brought Shon to prison as a teenager and destroyed his promising future. She crumbles

as Shon shows us what she has long known him to be—a extraordinarily gifted artist trapped by impossible circumstances:

> "When I play music nothing is closed to me. I'm not afraid of
> people and what they say. There's no war in music…. But when
> you leave your room… down in the street… it's war! People have
> hurt my feelings for years. I never forget. You can't get even
> with people by playing the fiddle. If music shot bullets I'd like
> it better."

++++

In the spring, I am offered two classes on a CUNY campus in midtown Manhattan. Although I have been teaching theatre for decades, I
am nervous when I first walk into the black-box theatre on an official
college campus as a "professor." After putting down chairs, laying out
materials, and propping the door open, I wait for the students to arrive.
I am going over my prep once again when I hear a familiar voice:

"Hey, Rich."

Standing in the door is Max, who played the lead son in our Ferrisburg production of *Fathers and Sons*, newly released and now enrolled
at CUNY. When he found out I was teaching on campus, he dropped
another class to take mine. I look up smiling and shake my head:

"Maxwell Jefferson, as I live and breathe."

Max and I had a running game while rehearsing *Fathers and Sons*.
Whenever I used a word that wasn't part of his vocabulary, he would
demand I give him the full definition and usage so he could record it
in his notebook. After a while I introduced certain words on purpose,
ones I thought he might like… *clandestine, inculcate, supercilious.* One

of his favorites was *neophyte*, constantly insisting that, after all the rehearsals and theatre classes he'd had inside, he could no longer be described in such terms.

As the other students start drifting into the room, I place the red X in the center of the space and call my first college class onto the floor. I look around the circle, my eyes finally resting on Max. It is a remarkable moment. Here we are, two men with completely different histories having life experiences for the first time—Max as a college student and me as a college professor—in the real world.

I introduce the first exercise and ask Max if he will start us off. He beams:

"Sure, Rich. It's not like I'm a neophyte!"

10

ACTING OUT

"Rich, wouldn't it be great if someday we could do this on the street?"

During class or rehearsal or in the middle of an exercise, someone will just blurt that out. I always nod and smile but find it somewhat akin it to the "pipe dreams" floating around Harry Hope's bar in O'Neill's *The Iceman Cometh*. But through the years, as the number of men released from prison steadily increases and contact with them becomes more frequent, the idea of forming a company of formerly incarcerated actors begins renting space in my head.

Whenever one of the men *is* released from prison, I am unsettled by my response. A day the men long for and fantasize about for an interminable time is one of resounding loss for the Theatre Workshop. The synergy and interdependence of the group members is precious, bonds not unlike those forged by soldiers in battle and addicts in recovery. My empathy for the man going home is inevitably tempered by the sadness that an integral member of our company will not be standing in the circle on Friday night. That melancholy leaves me feeling guilty as hell.

Occasionally, after they are released, I hire one of the guys for a reading or a demo, but the opportunities for reconnection are few and far between. I receive texts on holidays and Father's Day, but the weekly meetings, rehearsals, and shows that provided regularity of contact slowly diffuse into the universe.

The first guy to get out was Juice. Prior to my residency at Ferrisburg, Juice performed in a production of *Two Trains Running* directed by Larry and became a bit of a celebrity inside. He was released before *Tuf Love,* yet his brief time in the workshop made an impression, especially on his first day of class. I was conducting an improv exercise called "Whatever You Say," where the actor (or "victim," in this case) sits in a chair onstage and is subject to a barrage of questions and challenges that he cannot deny or refuse. The rule is to never say "No," to always go with what you are given in an improvisation so it can continue to develop. When I asked for a volunteer, Juice rocketed to the chair, not knowing that the first actor was a sacrificial lamb. I told Juice the exercise had already started, and he sat proud and pompous, ready to show off the ferocity for which he was known. I laid out the rules of Whatever You Say with great import and explained how difficult it could be at times. Then I pretended to remember something and turned to him:

"Wait a minute, haven't you done this before?"

"No! I never…"

He realized his gaffe as he made it. It is always an embarrassing moment for whoever gets caught, but was especially so for someone with his reputation. He worked through Kübler-Ross's 5 stages of grief in a nanosecond, smirked, and, shaking his head and fists, skulked back to his seat.

Juice contacts me through my website and suggests we grab a vegan pizza, his post-prison bow to better nutrition. I arrange to pick him up at the health club where he works as a trainer. I double-park out front and wait, a bit anxiously, not knowing what to expect. Juice cruises through a set of heavy glass doors and strolls toward my pickup truck wearing black sweats and a shit-eating grin. He climbs in the cab and snaps on his seatbelt:

"So, am I your first?"

He is indeed the first formerly incarcerated man I knew personally on the inside who is now out, and it is an awkwardly unawkward moment. The workshop no longer provides a *raison d'etre* and there is no common enemy against whom to rally, yet the connection is undeniable. Maybe all those rounds of Hello....

Juice's timing is perfect. I have a gig for him. I am directing the annual Random House Creative Writing Competition Awards Ceremony at Symphony Space and one of the dramatic pieces being staged is a scene between a young girl and a monk. Juice's austerity is perfect for the role, and the alopecia he developed while incarcerated has rendered him hairless. He looks as if he's stepped right out of Central Casting. He does a great job as the monk and consequently works the awards ceremony several years in a row. A great candidate for an outside class.

My right-hand man, Hector, who was indispensable in the workshop, is the second to be released. Dining on huevos rancheros at a coffee shop in Union Square, we discuss next steps. The Random House gig is getting bigger every year, and I need an assistant. Hector's administrative skills and resourcefulness (and his acting chops) land him the gig. A few months later, during a tech rehearsal in Symphony

Space's 700-seat proscenium theatre, I glimpse Hector giving instructions to some of the other technicians with a *real* iPad in his hand and I think back to the rudimentary materials he made work so well at Ferrisburg. Hector is a keeper.

A tall, imposing character who showed up at a rehearsal for *Inside Out* at Ferrisburg with the disclaimer that he was not a performer—he just wanted to "help out"—is my third contender. He had extensive technical experience, having run several talent shows and music recitals. I asked him his name:

"Reality."

I told him he was hired.

One year, Juice, Hector, and Reality are all working the Random House gig in various capacities. Several other paroled workshop members come to see the show and catch up with old friends. The men in the picture someone snaps out in front of Symphony Space look a lot more like a theatre troupe than a pipe dream. I think about the other guys whom I have worked with over the years—Wolf at the NYCAAPSE luncheon; Hector, Don, and Eddie at the Brooklyn Academy of Music; Micah and Frederick at Pace University; Billy's Off-Broadway run of *Holding*. It becomes increasingly clear that a new theatre workshop already exists Brigadoonishly on the outside. All we need is a home.

While studying with Mercedes Ruehl at HB Studio in Manhattan, I see that HB's wide range of programs could certainly fold in an acting class for the formerly incarcerated. I send a thirteen-minute trailer from *Showdown* to Edith Meeks, the executive and artistic director. She is moved by the video and requests a meeting. A series of planning sessions lead to a trial run—a showcase featuring Ferrisburg alumni to be presented in December 2019 at HB's Playwrights Theater on Bank Street. I round up the usual suspects.

Ma, I regret that you took my words as hurtful. Please believe me when I say that was not my intention and I'm sorry for any pain I caused. Sometimes I just want to feel a little extra love from you.

The evening opens with Hector's moving performance of a monologue from *Inside Out*—an aching letter written from his cell to his neglectful mother. Next is a screening of the video that has now become a signature piece for Acting Out. Although the clip is choppy and filled with coughs and echoes, its rough-hewn quality works in its favor, demonstrating the challenging circumstances under which the work was created. Two scenes from *This Is This* follow the video, and we close with "Let's Bounce" from *Showdown*, a tribute to Beckett's *Waiting for Godot*:

VICTOR
I love you.

ERNIE
(Pause) Okay.

VICTOR
What do you mean, okay?

ERNIE
Okay. I get it.

VICTOR
But do you feel it?

ERNIE
Do I "feel the love?"

VICTOR
Yeah.

ERNIE
(Pause) I don't know.

VICTOR
Too bad.

ERNIE
You know what I mean.

VICTOR
Unfortunately, I do.

ERNIE
It's hard.

VICTOR
I know.

ERNIE
Love.

VICTOR
Yeah.

Don and Na Sol, two veteran actors of theatre behind bars, play the scene simply and honestly, never falling into the traps often laid in absurdist comedies. Standing in the wings waiting for the curtain call, Van, who spent almost twenty years upstate, leans over and whispers: "This is dope!"

Our debut in HB's charming black-box theatre plays to a sold-out house. The talkback is vibrant, questions and answers and kudos colliding and overlapping for almost an hour. It is a remarkable coming together, much like the sessions after the prison shows. It is further heightened because this is the men's first performance where they are the "civilians" being recognized by a New York theatre community. Gratitude is felt on both sides of the footlights as the conversation ripples around the room. There is talk of redemption and rehabilitation, forgiveness and fighting the good fight, but the most poignant share of the evening comes from Don and has to do with a pair of jeans.

After his release, Don lived at a quasi–homeless shelter where I visited him several times. I'd bring coffee and donuts and we'd sit in a quietish corner in the visiting room where he brought me up to speed on his plans. Number one was getting out of the hellish place in which he was living: "Not really much different than jail, Rich."

I asked if there was anything he needed. He looked at the floor and blushed as deeply as his complexion would allow, his pride running interference with his gut. It seemed there was something he did not so much need as *want*. He smiled awkwardly:

"I haven't worn a pair of jeans in thirty years."

He explained that all he had were work pants for his porter job and a pair of slacks for job interviews, but nothing to kick around in. On my next visit I brought him two pairs.

During the HB showcase talkback, Don is fielding a question about reentry, how long it took him to feel like he was once again a part of society, when his throat begins to close. He cries as he describes slipping on his first pair of jeans in over three decades and how *that* was the moment that made him feel like he was back, that he was home, that he was free. He looks over at me with love and mischief and winks through his tears.

Don's theatre experience was extensive while incarcerated. He acted in many productions, wrote original material for the stage, and directed several plays including *A Soldier's Story* at a facility on Staten Island. Don's parting gift to the Theatre Workshop was some original material for *Inside Out*. The first, "Vendetta," an edgy scene between a jaded veteran and a rookie cop, fit nicely in the show, but the second piece, "The Box," a stinging castigation of solitary confinement, went beyond pushing the envelope—it obliterated it. The monologue was off-the-charts good, but Don and I both knew it would never make the cut at Ferrisburg. Don took it in stride and shrugged:

"Maybe on the outside."

I did give *The Box* a private staged reading in the workshop, however. I had a new guy, JJ, a terrific actor who was very vocal about the inhumanity of solitary confinement. He advocated for the abolishment of the practice and his rants were embraced by everyone who had lost friends to the Box. JJ often documented the untold numbers of men and women who were isolated in a tiny, windowless cell, twenty-three hours a day for weeks, months, years. I could only imagine what he would bring to it as an actor. The anticipation of a powerhouse performance eclipsed my fear or misgivings about taking the material back inside.

One Friday, I slipped *The Box* in with the sheaves of material in my bag, confident it would not be noticed during the cursory glance given by the officer in the arsenal.

Not this time. The new officer did not flip mindlessly through my papers like the others—he examined every page. After reading the first few lines of *The Box,* he ripped it out of the folder with the triumph of discovering contraband in a spot-check inspection. He shook his head and smiled smugly:

"The sergeant's gonna wanna see *this.*"

While I waited, the guard quoted lines from the piece to a colleague on break. There were a lot of "Whoa!"s and "Aw man!"s as he glanced my way, convinced he *had* me. During the lengthy wait for the sergeant, I feared he had. *What the hell was I thinking?* I knew the piece was inflammatory. I knew better than to poke the bear. I was putting the whole workshop in jeopardy to demonstrate my sympathy for the cause and be raptured by a theatrical turn.

When the sergeant arrived, he took the script from the guard, sat, and read the entire monologue. I was now convinced he would confiscate the material and dismiss me from the facility. When he finished reading, he slipped the piece back in the bag with my paperwork and shrugged at the guard:

"It's just a play, John."

From what tier of heaven he descended, I will never know.

I suspected more trouble in the classroom when JJ scanned *The Box* and shook his head with a cocky smile: "I dunno, Rich. *This* could be a problem... 'cause I'ma *do* it!"

JJ walked to the center of the room, dropped into a metal school desk chair, and shook his arms and legs as if to free himself from invisible restraints. He took a deep breath and bellowed the first line from his core:

"CO! ON THE LIGHTS! CO!! *ON THE FUCKIN' LIGHTS*!!"

We could hear the actual CO racing down the hall, the rubber soles of his work shoes slapping against the newly waxed floor. He burst in the room, stopping JJ as he took a deep breath: "WHAT in HELL is going on in here?"

I explained, in the words of the sergeant, that it was just a play and that we were good. He stared at me with a why-the-fuck-are-you-even-here look—a look to which I had become accustomed. He scanned the room, barked at a few of the men to remove their hats, checked that the bathroom door was locked, and exited stage left. As soon as the door closed, JJ turned to me and grinned:

"I told ya."

In my time at Ferrisburg, I often wander in and out of these gray areas—or even cross red lines—to demonstrate solidarity with the men while trying to adhere to the stringent guidelines of the prison. It unnerves me to even brush up against the rules, much less bend or break them, and I panic when I think I have gone too far and am risking it all for the sake of a telling moment. But my gut tells me to soldier on, that gently pushing back *is* an integral part of the work: not so much sleeping with the enemy as trying to occasionally wake them up.

++++

On January 19, 2020, with a small grant from the India Blake Foundation and HB's offer of a home space, we hold our first *outside* class almost ten years to the day that I first walked into Building 112 at

Ferrisburg. Standing in a circle around a small red X on the floor of the basement studio are Don, Hector, Wolf, Max, Horus, and Lew, among a range of familiar faces I've known from the workshop through the years. When we do Check-In, the responses range from "grateful" to "official" to "I don't fucking believe this!" Our castle in the air now has a foundation and we are, as miraculous as it seems, doing this stuff on the street.

Attendance is spotty the first few weeks, many of the men traveling from the far reaches of the boroughs and suburbs. The meeting time on Sunday morning conflicts with church for some of them, but there is a core group that is consistent and dedicated. A few new members find their way to us through postings on social media and chance encounters at parole reporting sites.

One day I answer a call from an unknown number. The raspy voice is unmistakable:

"Rich, it's Cisco. I just got out. Ran into Lew at parole. He told me about the class. I want in!"

Cisco was a member of the Ferrisburg Theatre Workshop for mere months, showing great promise until he went to the Box. Despite having no prior theatre background, Cisco was one of the most daring and committed members of the workshop. He is waiting outside HB studio for an hour on the first day of class.

Another surprise is Tyrique. Released in 2019, he runs into Max when reporting for parole and tags along with him to class. He appears as shy and cautious as he was his first day at Ferrisburg. His smile reveals the same broken tooth that caused an awkward and ice-breaking moment in the original workshop: in a scene from

Awake and Sing!, everyone laughed nervously when he blurted out his line: "All right, I can't get my teeth fixed!"

During a break in class, Tyrique gives his side of the story of being in the Box on opening night of *This Is This.* I am disquieted and moved when tells me how he recited the lines from his scenes the same night he was to have performed them with the rest of the cast.

Almost nine years earlier, Tunde was the first actor to step forward during *Tuf Love* and speak the opening line of the Actor's Vow: "I will take my rightful place on the stage, and I will be myself." It seems only fitting he should be one of the men standing in the circle at HB. Shortly afterward, he is arrested and detained by the Immigration and Customs Enforcement for a discrepancy in his citizenship status. Born on a US Army Base in Germany, Tunde's father, a Haitian national, was never able to complete the process of obtaining his US citizenship. The stringent laws of the new administration sweep Tunde up with thousands of others on what appears to be a xenophobic and punitive technicality. Tunde served twenty-four years for a crime he had only been a witness to, and now it seems could be deported to a country in which he has never lived. Losing men along the way is difficult, but these grave injustices—where a man, in essence, may lose the life for which he waited so long—are deeply disturbing. His case is still pending.

On the inside, everyone's commitment to the workshop is fortified by the fact that it is the only game in town. On the outside, the men are juggling jobs, families, the stringent restrictions of parole, and their battles against PTSD following their prison experience. Theatre is no longer a priority. Those who see it through, however, come to realize just what the exercises and technique training are inculcating—that they excel at this work, that they are good at what they do, that they are *good*. Nothing motivates a man more than the idea that what he is doing, and who he is, is valuable and appreciated and wanted.

A lifetime ago, during a rehearsal of a musical revue in high school, the director pulled me aside after my small song-and-dance turn and said something I was not used to hearing:

"You're really good at this stuff."

I stood there, baffled, as if he were speaking another language. He pressed on:

"You know that, right?"

It just did not compute. I was so crushed by my father's disparagement, and my mother had modeled a despair and resignation that made me question any adult who seemed to take me seriously. I did not trust compliments—from anyone. But my director insisted that I *say* it. That I was good at this stuff. How could I? It felt as if I were being asked to lie or turn state's evidence. I had always heard the opposite—that I was lazy, not tough enough, had my head in the clouds. But he stood there smiling, waiting, his eyes locked on me, until I did say it.

So many of the men in the workshop were severely damaged as children—by violence and abandonment and psychological abuse. By parents who forgot (or never knew) what it was like to be a child. By teachers who resented their students or were envious of them. By bullies so broken and frightened that their only option was to beat down everyone else around them. By a society and system of government that relegated them to second-class citizenship because of their skin color or accent or economic status. These created scars that prevented them from pursuing vocations, that marginalized and alienated them, that created a soul-sickness that resulted in trouble with school and work and the law.

But good turns have staying power as well—the kudos, the shows of good faith, the unconditional gestures of support and love. *I'm good at this stuff.* Saying that—being *made* to say that—is a game changer. I will always be grateful to the teachers and mentors who understood, who were not threatened by the raw talent and promise of youth, who knew how much a young person aches for acceptance and respect by a "grown-up."

Theatre, music, dance, and other fine arts need to be an integral part of our education systems, community centers, and families so that we can fix things. It is unsettling that these lifesaving outlets are the first to be eliminated when belts are tightened and budgets are cut. There is enormous hope in movements like the Ferrisburg Theatre Workshop, Acting Out, and many other like-minded arts organizations like Rehabilitation through the Arts, Justice Arts Coalition, and The Bard Prison Initiative. The struggle to keep these enterprises alive is worth every dime that sustains them. When an improv kicks off into high gear and everyone is "in the zone," freely associating and living joyously in the moment, we are all free. When the human connection in a scene is intense and genuine, it renews our hope for true communion with our friends (and enemies) on this planet. When the coda of prison production lifts everyone out of a crumbling gymnasium and into the Elysian Fields, it is a singular and priceless experience.

After our first month of class at HB, I offer to drop Lew in Harlem on my way home to Washington Heights. He climbs in the passenger seat, seemingly lost in thought, and then turns to me:

"Rich, I never realized just how *important* theatre is."

To say it is music to my ears would be an understatement. From the first time I saw a play, I knew how important it was, how I needed to be a part of it, and how much it was already a part of me. And here is someone, lost to the streets at thirteen, incarcerated for fifteen and a half years, who now knows that too. Lew is serious about acting. He takes auditions and is saving money for headshots. Like Billy, he is the exception, not the rule, in terms of seeking a career in the arts. But regardless of what opportunities may present themselves or pass him by, Lew has already succeeded. He has achieved something no Tony or Obie Award could ever effect—a change of heart. He now knows that what he has been seeing and saying and doing all his life need not be set in stone, that he can stop, turn, and step into a new dimension.

11

NO MAN IS AN ISLAND

Juan is one of the finest actors I ever had in the Ferrisburg workshop. He delivered a gripping performance in *Fathers and Sons* as the father who refuses to enable his drug-addicted son. Small, intense, committed, and unafraid to access emotions that might be perceived as weak in an oppressively male environment, Juan has never done the "Bio Bit" exercise, which I am using to gather material for our next show, *No Man Is an Island*. Bio Bits are an attempt to encapsulate one's life in a few minutes. Because of the time constraint, the actor tends to zero in on the most salient moments, often kicking up long-buried feelings. Even though Juan will not be in the cast of the upcoming production due to his imminent release, I want to give him an opportunity to experience the exercise before he leaves. I place a chair in the center of the room and nod for him to claim it. He sits and starts: "I was born in Mexico City...."

He tells us how, at four, his father brought him (illegally) to New York, then back to Mexico for a funeral, and then back to New York again. While in high school, Juan was determined to enlist in the Navy after graduation to "see the world," but the recruitment office told him he needed to apply for a passport since he did not have a green card. He was not close with his parents, feared their disapproval, and was unaware he could apply for the document on his own. Discouraged and seeing no hope in trying to better himself, he dropped out of high school, ended up on the streets, joined a gang, committed a crime, and spent twenty years behind bars.

While Juan recounts that pivotal moment, he seems to see for the first time how, due to fear and ignorance, not taking a simple action cost him two decades of his life. His sudden awareness of the gravely missed opportunity overwhelms him, undoubtedly compounded by the knowledge that once he is released from prison he will be deported to Mexico, a country he barely remembers. Juan drops his head back and looks up at the tin ceiling as tears course down past his ears and drop onto the floor. The men lean forward and let him cry, chanting softly:

"We got you, Juan. We got you."

No Man Is an Island, written and performed by the members of the workshop, is an evening of woven stories that trace the broad arc of each man's life from early childhood to the present; like Juan, they examine watershed moments in their lives while acknowledging along the way those they hurt, and those who hurt them. The show also acknowledges the sustaining relationships of family, friends, and, if relevant, a God of their understanding.

"What have you done right in your life?"

"What are you afraid of?"

"How are you helping others?"

"To whom do you need to apologize?"

"Who do you want to thank?"

"For what must you forgive yourself?"

"What do you have to live for?"

Writing prompts generate sheaves of material as I restructure our Friday-night sessions like with *Inside Out,* splitting the time between actor training and writing exercises. There are many constants in the men's compositions—the loss of parents during childhood, drugs, alcohol, and sexual abuse, neglect, foster care, the arrest of siblings, the murder of friends and relatives, quitting school, gang pressure, poverty, racism…. The steady barrage documents an existence that has long hung by a thread:

> I was born to a teenage mother and father whose parents had to raise me, then I became a teenager, shot in the head, cuffed to a hospital bed, then chains embraced me, bars and barbed wire fences hugging 'cause I wasn't hugged enough… this child, that child, this mouth, that mouth, which house to lay down and dream, which route to walk where my soul could stay clean, which route could I walk where my soles could stay clean. All I wanted was love, but discipline received, forced responsibilities and unanswered questions answered by dealers and pimps, big time and simps, killers that smiled… what do I believe from where life's lessons confused, etched in my mind… new shoes, fly, tough, don't get abused… What I seen my mother go through— Shit! Attempted suicide, jail, cut, raped, HIV-positive—yet she

loves so strong with an enormous spirit—you can't help but smile. I just want to help her—be there for her—have enough money so she don't have to worry... but what about me?

When I lead off a writing session with the question "What is your favorite childhood memory?", the results are beautiful and loving portraits of grandparents, aunts, uncles, and parents who did the best with what they had, who managed to provide genuine moments of happiness for their sons and grandsons and nephews. Many of these memories are long-hidden until a simple cue releases recollections of goodwill and treasured experiences:

"Wanting an outfit for my birthday and my mother
   took the last of her money to get me one."
"Kissing Amy Santiago in the coat closet in third grade."
"Being with my father at his job, going to lunch together."
"Staying up late at night with my cousins at my grandmother's
   house playing Uno, Monopoly, and doing pranks on my uncle."
"Competing against five hundred students for the top ninety spots
   to receive college credits at F.I.T. and coming in thirty-seventh."
"When me, my sister, and mother had no food, but we had so
   much love for one another we didn't care about being hungry."
"My time on Culebra, where my mind was so clear and
   everything was so vivid and my life was so full of wonder."

One man's testament to his grandmother fills the room with identification:

Every Christmas she would drive from Albany to Newark in her Cadillac with her car packed so tight with presents that she could barely move inside the vehicle. My mom and dad were drug addicts and didn't give us much. My Grandma knew if she didn't bring us presents, we wouldn't get any. So she would have Christmas with her upstate family on the 24th and, no matter what, be in Newark on December 25th so that my sister and I could be children.

No man is an island. Whenever I sit in a theatre watching a play, I am grateful for the hundreds of hands and eyes and ears and voices that go into creating it. I am grateful for the playwright's choice to not just entertain but educate and enlighten. Here I am, in a roomful of men living under woeful circumstances, separated from those they love, confined to a space filled with fear and anger and resentment, and they choose to do the same thing. To give up Friday Movie Night and rec time and phone calls. To put off relaxing or sleeping after a grueling week of work and march down the crumbling macadam road to Building 112 to write and train and rehearse. To refuse to isolate or zone out, but rather connect with their fellows, share their thoughts and feelings, take emotional risks, laugh, cry, and work together to create something they hope will touch others. To send a message that they care about the world in which they live, those they love, and those they do not even know. To embrace the idea that by helping others they are also helping themselves.

No man is an island,
Entire of itself;

Every man is a piece of the continent,

A part of the main...

I bring in copies of John Donne's poem and give each man the opportunity, as with The Actor's Vow, to speak the speech for his fellows. And then, in one of the most potent writing exercises, I ask the men to pray—on paper: to write out their thoughts and feelings and petitions to a supreme being:

"I cry out to you in sadness and glory."

"I await my resurrection."

"If everything is providence then I'm sure you're going to remove these things that cause me to fail."

"I ask that you protect me from anything that will stop me from being released between now and then."

"I ask forgiveness for all the wrong that I have done to myself and others."

"May I mean well for all those who mean well for me, and may I be able to understand those who don't mean well for me."

"I pray for unconditional love, not a mere kiss and a hug."

"I want to be free, free of stress and the agony I go through daily, I want to be free, free to regain everything I've lost and give back to those who've helped me make it."

The spoken-word emcee of *This Is This*, Lanford—jailed for twenty-five years for a crime for which he will be later exonerated—says the exercise is too personal. He tells me he has an issue with writing about his relationship with a higher power. I encourage him to write about *that* instead. He is the last to turn in his work. His non-prayer proves to be the most supplicative of all:

> Why would I break a sacred vow and allow my prayer to become something utilized to invoke unknown responses from others? Do you not realize how much value lives within prayer or perhaps some of you may be unconvinced when sweat overlaps the brow and conjoins with tears that fall from my eyes when others utilized my addiction in order to paint a picture of me being the guy, did anyone stand up and say NO don't do that to him, no they turned their face and left me to struggle, knew I was innocent but wanted no trouble.

On Wednesday, March 11, 2020, I receive notice that CUNY campus classes are suspended indefinitely because of the COVID-19 pandemic. I expect a call from Ferrisburg the same day, but it does not come. Never imagining how the crisis will play out, I adopt the same attitude as with the snowstorm during *Inside Out* rehearsals and make the regular Friday trek upstate. At every stage of processing, I expect a "Wait" or "Stop," but the only change in routine is my having to sign a form stating I have not been sick nor in contact with anyone who is symptomatic. After executing the document, I am scanned, searched, stamped, and buzzed through the door as usual. There is no hard evidence of what is to come, save perhaps a slight tension in the corners of everyone's eyes.

Arriving at Building 112, I whisk past the guard at the front desk and head toward Room 8. Hearing voices echoing out into the hallway, I assume everyone is getting the room set up for class. I open the door to find only three men huddled in the corner. They turn with a jolt, obviously surprised to see me, and shout in unison: "Rich!"

The men explain that, since CUNY classes were suspended midweek, everyone thought the workshop would be canceled as well. I ask why, if that were the case, they are here. One of the guy shrugs:

"Just hopin'."

In all the years I have led the workshop, I rarely cancel classes. If I have an unavoidable conflict, I call the prison immediately. In class, I make it clear that a no-show on my part would be due to extraordinary and unavoidable circumstances. That point of procedure became a hard promise after Clay's mother pulled me aside at one of the family performances and squeezed my hand between hers:

"My son *lives* for Friday night."

When I do have to call in, however, the prison's nondisclosure policy prevents the officials from telling the men why. All they get is: "He's not coming."

As rejection and dismissal are things they have come to expect, it takes months, sometimes years, before new members drop their guard and trust that someone has their back. In the early days I feared the prison's non-explanation for an absence would be perceived as a who-the-fuck-cares gesture on my part.

My mother died on a Thursday, the day before workshop. Ferrisburg was my first call. For once, perhaps due to the solemnity of the occasion, they told the guys why I was not coming in. But they got it wrong. They said my *father* had died. The men knew my dad had been gone for decades and that my mom was sick, so they figured it out, inured to the careless and erroneous way that vital information is often communicated to them.

When I returned to class the following week, a queue slowly formed as I walked in the door. Each man waited silently to shake my hand and express his condolences. I felt far more consoled, standing at the head of that awkward little line, that at any time during the wake and funeral when I was surrounded by relatives and friends.

Earlier that year, when my mom had taken ill, I mentioned it to the men. The following week I received a Get Well card purchased from the commissary, each man having scribbled his best wishes inside. Along with the card was a paper rose that one of the men had crafted—from toilet tissue!

Volunteers are not allowed to exchange any form of written communication without express permission from prison officials. After a production, the many cards and thank-you letters for me and members of the civilian production team are processed by the deputy of programs, who inspects them, removes any disallowed items, and deposits them at the arsenal for pickup on the way out. I am so grateful that both the card and gift made it through the process. My mom was deeply moved by their sentiments—and thrilled with the rose.

March 13 is the last in-person class I will teach for almost three years, and it is the smallest of circles that forms around the X that evening. To augment the group, we commandeer the porter on duty to join us after he finishes mopping the hall and emptying the trash. That evening the Hello exercise resonates more than ever, not by what is said, but what is not. The most poignant moment in the exercise occurs when I reprise a dialogue I used when my friend Judy visited the workshop a few years ago.

Prior to the start of class, Jake had thanked Judy for taking the time to come into the facility, to share her time and talent with them. He was standing on the X when Judy walked into the circle, looked up, and spoke the first line with great sincerity:

"I'll never forget you."

He looked at her, smiled sadly, and answered:

"Yes, you will."

Although it was a set response to a scripted prompt, it was informed by the innate acceptance of myriad disappointments. As Judy choked back tears, Jake returned to the circle and she took his place on the X. When the next actor walked in and said "I'll never forget you" to my sobbing colleague, genuinely sympathetic to her emotional state, her response—"Yes, you will"—was heartbreaking.

Repeating that dialogue on March 13, 2020, portends the isolation that is about to descend upon us. It is also a prescient suggestion that the world will not learn anything from it.

The following Monday volunteer services are terminated until further notice. *No Man Is an Island* closes before it opens. The following weeks are filled with harrowing reports of how fast the virus spreads through prisons, especially ones like Ferrisburg, where the men live in huge dorms much like homeless shelters. Since masks are forbidden for security reasons—the prisoner's identities must be clear at all times—the transmission of the deadly virus is rapid and extensive. Not only do most people not consider the plight of the incarcerated during this crisis, many shrug it off, as if these lives were expendable. I am reminded of Raul's unforgiving comment about bad people getting what they deserve. Although the pervasiveness of the pandemic inside the prison is alarming, this disregard stuns and saddens me. The faces and voices and histories of these men have truly touched me. They have shared their thoughts and fears with me. I have watched them own their errant behavior and rebuild their characters. They have proven themselves to be valuable and precious souls—souls that are now in peril.

What follows is my longest absence from Ferrisburg in over a decade. I miss the men, I miss the work, but most of all I miss *it*—that mysterious field of energy that fills a simple classroom in one of the most unlikely places on earth with an abundance of hope and love. I miss that part of me that is revealed there more than anywhere else—the courage I have, the faith I find, the assurance that what I am doing matters.

Maybe *No Man Is an Island* will play the theatre-in-the-gym at Ferrisburg one day, a new group of actors adding their voices and stories, infusing it with lessons learned from the unfathomable experience we are about to live through. Maybe the universal fear and grief that surrounds us will elevate the play, demonstrate that life-saving gestures are born of humility and sacrifice. That if the touch of a hand or the intake of breath endangers a life, we must put aside our pride and do whatever is necessary to protect each other. That we must heed John Donne's testimony:

Any man's death diminishes me,
Because I am involved in mankind.

12

TALK TO ME

"You know what's the matter with you people? All of you? You're not brave enough. That's right... like in the old flicks...."

...

"Wait, hold up. He's frozen."

"Cisco, can you hear me? You're frozen."

"He can't hear you."

"Oh God, what are we gonna... Make an announcement? Or just wait?"

"I fucking hate this!"

"You're not muted!"

"Wait, you mean they...? Shit!"

"MUTE!"

"I'm sorry, I didn't..."

"Hold on, I think it's working again... Cisco, can you hear me?"

When Acting Out, our fledgling company of formerly incarcerated actors, resumes meeting on Zoom, we have no idea what we're doing but are hell-bent on doing it anyway. Our launch is anything but adroit. Besides my complete inexperience in teaching or directing online, most of the men do not have laptops or computers and their only link is a cell phone, oftentimes an older, less adaptive model. Many have poor Wi-Fi connections or none at all. They need to relocate to other apartments and workspaces to grab a signal, and even then it is often lost during rehearsal. Because of cramped living conditions, it is difficult for the men to have privacy. Interruptions are constant—dogs, cats, children running in and out of the frame, disgruntled wives and partners toe-tapping for attention, televisions and video games bleeding into the virtual room.

In the early days of the pandemic, I attend a Zoom music recital for students enrolled at a prestigious private school on the Upper East Side of Manhattan. I am struck by the stark difference—private dedicated spaces, good light, excellent wireless connections, full-screen views. No amount of rhetoric about the disparity of the haves and have-nots could make it any clearer. I cannot help but think about the deficits many of these men suffered in childhood far beyond technological amenities: the basic human comforts of peace and quiet and a space to call their own.

In the early weeks at HB Studio, I assigned monologues that sometimes dealt with uncomfortable and painful events—the rejection of a child, the loss of a friend or sibling, the absence of a parent, a secret passion, the humiliation of being *other*, the acknowledgment of true feelings. It was remarkable how quickly the men reached a point of inevitability with the monologues, how deftly they climbed into the character and made the playwright's words their own.

Before the shutdown, I had planned to remount *Fathers and Sons* at HB in December of 2020 as our debut production. With HB closed, I have to switch things up. I tell the men to continue working on their monologues until we get sorted. To Zoom or not to Zoom, that is the question. The men are down for doing a show, and when HB offers us a virtual platform, I come up with a plan. I arrange thirteen monologues into four ascending sections and call it *Talk to Me.*

There are two incredible reunions. The first is with Juan, who moved everyone to tears in his last class and was then deported to Mexico upon his release from prison in 2019. Prior to his incarceration, Juan had grown up in the Bronx (just a subway ride from HB) and was a prime candidate for Acting Out. His deportation was a bitter disappointment to the company and a devastating blow to him. A few weeks after Acting Out began meeting at HB, before the shutdown, I received a text from Juan asking if he could obtain a copy of his scene from *Fathers and Sons*. On an itinerant job in Mexico City, he befriended a television producer who, intrigued by Juan's acting work in prison, asked for a reel. I had called my editor immediately and arranged to have the clip made. Now it hits me: Juan *can* join the company now—online.

When Juan starts class, he is living on his father's farm outside a small pueblo in the heart of Mexico. Far from any major cities, the only public Wi-Fi modem is mounted on a water tower in the center of town. Over-trafficked and poorly maintained, the signal often freezes or drops out completely. Juan makes a deal with a friend who runs a small *farmacia* with dedicated cable who agrees to let him access her signal from a corner of the store. He is completely unbothered by the customers who come in and out for prescriptions and supplies while he is in class. All he cares about was that he is back in workshop! When the store is closed, Juan attends class from the roof of his uncle's barn, where he can pick up a stronger signal from the water tower. His tenacity in staying connected is impressive and the interruptions that beset him more amusing than annoying: goats bleating, roosters crowing, mariachi bands wandering in and out of town, the popping and whizzing of fireworks celebrating traditional holidays.

During rehearsals, Juan sends me a video recording of the monologue he will be performing in *Talk to Me*. He is standing in front of a rough-hewn fence on his farm, cattle grazing in the distance. It is raining. He appears to look *through* the camera as he shows us the transformation that has taken place, the man that he has become:

> I got lucky… found somebody I could talk to, and let some of the shit that was eatin' me alive out. It didn't happen overnight but after a while I started to realize that my fear and anger and laziness and depression was from bein' beaten down when I was a kid, that it wasn't my fault and I had to learn how to start trustin' people again. That there are decent people out there… maybe I'm even one of them.

Eddie D. debuted onstage in *Tuf Love*. I cast him in a scene from *American Buffalo*, not just for the quiet threat his three hundred pounds brought to the scene, but for the keen focus and inherent gentility that tempered his imposing figure.

I am shocked and saddened to learn that Eddie is now languishing in a nursing home due to a freak fall that severed his spinal cord and left him paraplegic. But again, Acting Out is now accessible to him. Eddie fights back tears as I welcome him back into the company. I assign him a monologue from Odets's *Paradise Lost*. Undaunted by the nurses walking in and out of the frame, the ambient sound of multiple

TVs, the clattering of food trays, and the buzz of nearby phone conversations, Eddie, propped up by extra pillows in his hospital bed, takes us all to task, demonstrating a steely courage in the face of the cards he has been dealt.

> No, there is more to life than this.... The past was a dream. But this is real! To know from this that something must be done.... Everywhere now men are rising from their sleep. Men, men are understanding the bitter black total of their lives. Their whispers are growing to shouts! They become an ocean of understanding! No man fights alone!

I underestimate the power *Talk to Me* has on the audience. We are held over for the entire summer, performing to robust virtual houses. The talkbacks are emotional and filled with love and appreciation. We hear the same thing over and over: most viewers think the monologues are original. The actors live so beautifully in the literature, hold the lives of the characters so close to their chests, are so *inevitable*, that each of the pieces—many of which are masterworks by major playwrights—come across as their own stories.

When the murder of George Floyd and the racial protests it foments eclipse the pandemic and the ongoing political chaos, *Talk to Me* becomes even more relevant, not necessarily for what is being said, but by who is saying it, as Acting Out's press release makes clear:

> The cumulative impact of the individual performances is powerful and emotional, unintentionally resonating with the global pandemic and widespread protests. The cast itself, a stirring consequence of mass incarceration, is entirely African American and

Latino. Clifford Odets, Robert Anderson, August Wilson, and Tennessee Williams have never felt more relevant, more universal than when performed by these men who amongst them have accrued over a century of time behind bars. Oscar and Tony Award winner Mercedes Ruehl, in response to their work, was effusive: "So profound and wrenching they will stop you in your tracks with their glory."

That release is superseded by an email from KJ Steinberg, coproducer and writer of NBC's hit show *This Is Us*, after seeing *Talk to Me*:

There was something so unintentionally beautiful and raw and exposing, seeing the actors in their kitchens, their hospital beds, their cars... their lives. The REALNESS—faces so close you could see every thought, every tear that was held back, every flit of anger behind the eyes. It was a truly singular experience.... it just felt especially poignant during this time of isolation, to be allowed into the hearts of strangers so generously. During this time when we're pouring into the streets, yelling behind masks, faceless in our cries for justice. It was comforting frankly, and yes, empowering to see the FULL faces of courage and strength and hope.

Despite the glowing reviews and great audiences, it is still anyone's guess as to what will go wrong, technically, at each live show. Wi-Fi connections are severed, actors forget to unmute themselves, audience members disrupt the flow of the piece with live chats and comments that *should* be muted, screen sharing malfunctions, sound cues inexplicably go silent. Still, audiences are forgiving, and the men are undaunted. One of the guys remarks after a technologically problematic show:

"After doin' thirty-one years in prison? That was nothin'."

The revolving door of actors continues as we encounter new obstacles and adapt to unprecedented circumstances. The technical difficulties and self-consciousness of the virtual platform expose insecurities and create tension. We lose three members after *Talk to Me.*

"I can't do it no more, Rich… the computer thing. I'll come back when HB opens again. When we do it for real."

Hampered by a learning disability and no experience with technology, Cisco simply books. Happily, he will return several years later when we remount *This Is This* at HB Studio, impressing his girlfriend and childhood buddies with a slick performance as Kewpie in a scene from *Paradise Lost.*

Horus and I became friends after he covertly reeled me back to Ferrisburg. During a brief hiatus I took due to other theatre work, I received an email from his brother, reporting that Horus and the guys at Ferrisburg were still meeting every Friday on their own, practicing monologues and running through the exercises I taught them. Putting that image in my mind was a cheap shot, but it worked. I returned shortly thereafter.

During *Talk to Me,* Horus becomes increasingly testy during tech and pickup rehearsals and seems annoyed when the show is repeatedly extended. He resigns an hour after the final performance via an e-card. He acknowledges his love of the camaraderie both inside and out, the integrity of the work and material, but now that he is pursuing the social work he had always wanted to do, it is time for him to go. He closes his note with the most telling admission of all:

"For so long I just couldn't leave.... All those years you came in, Rich, I didn't want you to think I didn't appreciate you."

Horus's stubborn loyalty to our friendship almost ruined it as I have become increasingly disturbed by his resentful attitude and ornery behavior. But once he comes clean, we are good.

Chill's departure is much more thorny—and upsetting. Chill has always been a little standoffish. He is not an alumnus of Ferrisburg but came recommended by Lew, who knew him from the neighborhood. During the production, Chill's performance, once engaging and energetic, becomes rote. He logs off immediately after the show and rarely sticks around for the talkback or notes. I soon learn that it has stemmed from a misunderstanding, a lost check, and a lifetime of mistrust and hurt feelings.

Most of the men receive their stipends electronically, but since Chill does not have a bank account, I have sent him a paper check weekly. One day he calls to say he has not received his most recent stipend. I ask him to wait a little longer, and that if it doesn't arrive in a few days, I'll issue a new one. He calls a few days later to say he still hasn't gotten it, so I replace the check. Then, inexplicably, his performance becomes even more dispirited. When I question him about it, he explodes, accusing me of never having mailed his original check, of having lied to him. I am nonplussed: "Chill, *why* would I do that?"

Later, I receive a USPS sleeve in the mail, containing the first check inside a damaged envelope. I notice that when the post office readdressed the envelope, they erred in copying his address, hence its being returned to me. I text Chill a picture of the envelope, hoping this will convince him once and for all there had been no deception. When I follow up with a call, it makes him even angrier. He insists over and over that I lied. I tell him that if he does not trust me, it will make it difficult to continue working together. He takes his cue:

"Right. I'ma leave the company."

And he is gone. I stand there staring at "Call Ended" on my phone and wonder what the hell happened. Then Lew's comment, made while rubbing his forearm, comes back to haunt me: I don't have *this*. For most of my adult life I have worked primarily with kids and adults of color. I am all too aware of the inequities and distrust that stem from our society's obsession with pigmentation. I have worked in the substandard schools and crime-ridden neighborhoods in which my students live. I have watched kids drop out because of pregnancy, family tragedies, gangs, and drug addiction. I have sat and listened to incarcerated men tell their stories, saddened by their never having been given a chance because of their race and social status. But I do not know, nor will I ever know what it is like to be a person of color in this country. I will never know the passes I have been given and the privilege I have had. I will never know the depths of the injustices that have been deliberately and unconsciously dealt to black and brown people by men and women who look like me. I will never be able to make Chill believe that I did not lie to him because he, and people like him, have been lied to for centuries.

I am grateful that most of my actors trust me enough to take the risk, to drop their guard, to make a fundamental shift in their relationship to the world and to people who may look like the enemy but are not. I will never be able to make it right with Chill or anyone who has been too fucked over to ever trust someone who looks like me. But it will not stop me from doing the work I love. It will not stop me from sharing this gift with those who are able and willing to accept it.

13

KID STUFF

CO, turn off the damn lights! I'm ready to take it down, and go
to rest, and these assholes wanna play games and keep fucking
with me. Think they can break me... "Abandon all hope, ye
who enter here." I remember reading this shit somewhere. It
sho' nuff applies to this shithole they call prison, or as that
white dude Abbott what's-his-face said about prison, "The
Belly of the Beast."

"The Box," the controversial monologue that never made it into the
original production of *Inside Out*, is the centerpiece of Acting Out's
remount of the show online six years later. No longer under the scru-
tiny of prison officials, Don's searing indictment of solitary confinement shocks and educates audiences as they sit in the comfort of their
living rooms.

Don and I earlier agreed that Lew was the man to play Vernon
in "The Box," having the power, anger, and tattoos for it. Lew kills
it every time—ranting and fuming as he accosts unseen COs and the
prison system at large. In the final performance, however, he steps into

another dimension. He goes back, *is* back in the Box as he had been so many times during his fifteen and a half years of jail time. He exposes a desperation we have not seen before as he clutches a wrinkled piece of paper bearing the scribblings of his rage and intelligence. He shows us just how much he hurts, how deep the humiliation and misery of solitary is. He uses every fragment of his shattered dignity to plead an impossible case from one of the most inhumane places created by man.

Yeah, I see what all this shit is really about, all this mass incarceration bullshit. It ain't no different when good ol' Uncle Sam ran up in Afghanistan laying his gangster down and calling it a regime change. This ain't nothing but a re-mix of slavery, with a touch of the Black Codes tossed in.... Some self-righteous, pompous-ass judge tells the white boy, "Now, Johnny you go on home and behave yourself," while he tells a brother, "Remand!" That shit started in the late 1800s and still goin' on.

For once, the medium to which he is consigned works *for* him. It is unsettling to watch Lew trapped in a literal box—trying to get out of it, get off the screen, out of solitary, of prison, of himself—to try and return to a world that seems to never have wanted him there in the first place. At the end of "The Box," the offstage CO finally heeds Lew's pleas to turn off the lights. From a blackened screen we hear Lew's howling from a virtual void, a chilling dispatch of terror and isolation. "The Box" closes with a steel door slamming shut, the reverberation of metal on metal, and then Landon's voice seeping out of the darkness:

They strayed us away from your dreams
by providing the people with the means to be fiends

those collective of hands fell over triple beams
while those role models that's claimed are in the music stream
coincidentally singing it was all a dream.

His tribute to Martin Luther King, Jr. is not a salve for what we have just witnessed but rather a bracing for the finale, "The Dilemma," a rendering of an imagined parole hearing that, like in the original, ends the show. When "The Dilemma" was staged at Ferrisburg, the chorus was physically present onstage in a kind of jury box, shadowing the character Davis, who sat before the board. In the online version, only Didier—playing Davis—appears on screen. As the disembodied voices of the commissioners poke and prod Davis, and the unseen phantom chorus echoes his responses with details of their own stories, you can feel Davis's inner turmoil in a deeply personal way.

2ND COMM. (offstage)
How old is your daughter?

DAVIS
17 ...

CHORUS
... 12 ... 9 ... 14 ... 8 months ... 1 and a half...

2ND COMM. (offstage)
You've been in prison her whole life. How old are you?

DAVIS
35 ...

CHORUS

... 37 ... 49 ... 60 ... 33 ... 28 ...

When granted a few last words by the commissioners, Davis expresses his remorse for his crime and, in a last plea for sympathy, states the years he has served to date. Then, one at a time, each formerly incarcerated actor appears in a box and announces the number of years he has been incarcerated. The screen is soon filled with the faces of men who have collectively served almost two hundred years in prison. It is not a political statement or plea for sympathy; it is a statement of fact. Once the entire cast is visible, one by one, they say their real names and release dates, and then disappear into the ether, leaving Davis alone. As the opening bars of Eminem's "Cinderella Man" fade in, Didier drops the Davis character and tells us *his* name and release date. His smile is undefinable in origin.

Inside Out is more than a noble experiment—it is a lumbering step forward that pushes the limits of an online platform to cast a harsh light on the reality of prison. And though we are once again beset with an abundance of technical malfunctions and human errors, I begin to heed our previous audiences to not only forgive but ignore what amounts to unavoidable rips and tears in the fabric we have sewn. I come to consider that perhaps everyone is held rapt by the production not despite its defects, but *because* of them.

++++

For three years I taught an acting class at a high school in the South Bronx to a freshman class of boys who had been culled from the general population because of their disruptive behavior. The class was a resounding success, thoroughly engaging the recalcitrant ninth graders and culminating in an afternoon of tightly acted scenes that left everyone's jaws dropped. Long before the enthusiastic curtain call, I knew it was a success when Wilson, one of the toughest kids in the class, leaned over to my assistant before the performance and whispered:

"Miss, I'm scared."

When word got out that I would be teaching the class again the following year, there was a protest from the girls who often chanted in the hall outside our classroom:

"We can be as bad as the boys! We can *act out* too!"

There was a perception that being bad was not only good—it was a prerequisite for the class! The girls were determined not to let the boys co-opt that territory. They prevailed.

Since the inception of Acting Out I have wanted to include women in the company, but I have not had any connections since I've only worked with men. When I make some inquiries at facilities and support groups for formerly incarcerated women, several candidates come knocking at our virtual door immediately. I fear the online version of the class might be off-putting to new members but, much like the girls in the South Bronx, these women want in, now.

The energy and perspective the women bring to Acting Out is refreshing and invigorating. The exercises and scene work are enhanced by the new yin and yang of the company, and the men are visibly impressed—sometimes even a bit intimidated—by the fearlessness and ferocity of our new members. An improv between two guys that begins with the line "Where the hell you been?" usually ends up being a bro brawl about owed money or a misadventure involving a woman. Don is completely unprepared for Tanya's response:

Where the hell I been? Where the hell YOU been at? I got two kids screaming for their Daddy who been MIA for a minute! I told you I ain't playin no more... I told you I'ma haul your dead-beat ass to court if you don't face facts and represent! And don't you start that cryin' shit neither. Who I look like, your momma?

Our third online production, *Kid Stuff*, is a series of monologues created from key events in the actors' childhoods. Each man and woman recalls a moment from their past and allows us to witness the ongoing transition as they come to grips with painful memories, lost loves, difficult decisions, moments of clarity, and the years of hard work that brought them to where they are now. Some recollections are endearing—winning a writing contest, learning to swim or do back-flips, having a surprise birthday party, taking the girl of one's dreams to the prom. Others are painful—a father leading his son into a life of crime, witnessing a mother's beating, being thrown out of the house, choosing between stealing and starving, having *both* parents in prison. The cast reconstitutes the disparate pieces of their lives while standing front and center as the honest and dignified people they have become.

When I was really, really young... there was an accumulation of things and I just didn't feel like they were right. Like things were not like they should have been, that things were wrong. And they definitely were. When I was locked up, I wasn't comforted by memories. Though I always had hope of returning to my family and friends. But relying on my memories of my youth to pass the time in jail? That wasn't something I did. What did I

A young man recounts the harrowing experience of attending his grandfather's funeral in shackles, where he confronts his estranged father and his beloved grandmother who no longer recognizes him due to dementia, in *Kid Stuff*. **Nira Burstein / Courtesy of Stopped Clock Films.**

want to be when I was kid? Honestly, I can't say. There wasn't really something I was striving to be. I didn't want to be poor. That's what I didn't want to be. But what I wanted to be... I can't tell you.

Tanya writes a monologue for the show that centers around a painful rejection by her mother. In rehearsal, when an emotion surfaces, she pushes it away, gets defensive, or starts laughing. I insist she drop her guard, feel what she is feeling, let us in. She throws up her hands:

"No! I can't do this! I don't even know if I can do the show! I don't want to feel these things!"

We both sit quietly for a while, watching each other's screens. I have always admired Tanya's social activism and prison reform work, her passion for making a difference in an indifferent world, but I have

Kid Stuff was the first production that brought formerly incarcerated women into the company, upping the emotional ante, as seen in this compelling monologue about a young woman whose father parented her from his prison to hers. **Nira Burstein / Courtesy of Stopped Clock Films.**

never told her as much. So, now I do. She thaws. I tell her *nobody* wants to feel the things in her monologue, but that artists—actors— have a responsibility to do that for those who cannot or will not feel them. I tell her that when we hold up a mirror to the audience so they can see themselves, we help them break through barriers, change, grow, be more fully human—that *that* is activism at its finest. She climbs back in the ring and faces her demons:

> The worst thing that ever happened to me was when I ran away
> and my mother wouldn't let me come back home. I was like 12
> and I lived in the street going from friend to friend and aunt to
> aunt. I think if she had let me come home, I may not have gone
> through a lot of the stuff that I went through, you know? Years

and years of incarceration because you don't have another way of expressing yourself.

Then she really goes there, says what she has wanted to say for so long:

I want to be a mom... Not having children really affects me. I'd be a cooking, cussing-ass mom that ain't scared to do nothing with their kids, like y'all want to go bungee jumping, let's go! My kids would always feel loved, because I would always have my hands on them—kissing them, loving on them. I would be the mom that drives the limo to the prom. I would be the mom you can tell anything to. I would be the mom you can trust.

The men and women in Acting Out are piecing together deeply fragmented lives. They are returning from a place that most of us cannot even imagine going. People who have been severely punished for long periods of time understand something that no lecture or sermon could ever begin to address. And when they step into the light and walk us through some of the most agonizing and personal moments in their lives, they are not just telling stories. They are showing us how to live. They are proof that no one is a lost cause, that we can start over at any point, that *we* are our greatest resource, our only hope:

Life is not what you're being taught it is. You learn to live life on your own as you grow. And life can be so much better, but that's a choice, and it's up to you to make these things happen. As difficult as life can be, it can be so much better. And we just have to learn how to not give up on ourselves. Because nobody's gonna teach you how to live life and nobody's gonna live life for you.

"Hector", in a tender monologue about going to the prom with the girl of his dreams in *Kid Stuff*. **Nira Burstein / Courtesy of Stopped Clock Films.**

This, from CJ, who lost custody of his son after serving seven years for a crime he did not commit. *Kid Stuff* closes with a monologue CJ wrote on his phone:

I've always had this dream, that I'm on a white sandy beach, and that the beach is my home. It's never the same dream.

But it's always similar, in that I'm near an ocean with crystal-clear blue waters. And I see myself walking on this beach... in peace.

14

WORKING CLASS

The 2021 Acting Out revival of my first Off-Broadway solo show—
Working Class—is our fourth online production. It not only shines a
dual light on working folks and the incarcerated, it addresses a major
shortcoming of the original show: the lack of diversity. In a one-person
show what you see is what you get—one race, one gender, one body
type. When I assign eight members of Acting Out one monologue
each, it instantly peoples the show with a broader and more inclusive
range of humanity.

When people ask me why my actors are so genuine, I say it's
because they have so few bad habits—bad *actor* habits. Having been
wronged as well as having done wrong, spending a lifetime trying to
find a way in, they have gained access to a nexus that links the core of
their pain and sensibilities to that of the character they are playing. In
Working Class, it is fascinating to watch their life experiences actualize
their performances. It's Stanislavsky on steroids.

When Sheri anguishes over the embarrassment she feels being
perceived as a trashy waitress by attendees at a wake for a truck driver
who was kind to her, she accesses the feelings of unworthiness she felt

in foster care, and then later in her difficult reentry from prison. When Eddie inveighs against the system because of repeated job losses, he unearths a justifiable rage over a lifetime of battling bigotry and racism. When Wolf, in a piece about an ex-con construction worker, confesses to being the victim of sexual assault in prison, he is electrifying in his disclosure, considering the extenuating and imagined circumstances of his twenty-year bid.

Juan plays a street vendor whose five-year-old daughter is dying of cancer. He works in a huge orange-shaped kiosk selling juice and snacks, rushing back and forth to the hospital to be with his daughter. As the absurdity of his workplace collides with his heartbreaking loss, he smashes through the two-dimensional medium, his tears running hot:

I don't want to work in this orange no more! I like to walk away from here right now! I like to run! Away from this thing and these problems and what this doctor is told me! I don't want nothing to do with this orange no more! I hate this goddamn thing!!

It's all there—the stupid mistake he made resulting in his twenty years behind bars; his deportation to a small pueblo in Nowhere, Mexico, where he does not have access to educational opportunities or the pursuit of the soul-satisfying work he found in jail; his inability to help his young nephews in New York, who he fears are now walking down the path that led him to hell.

Don closes the show with a portrayal of a high school dropout qualifying at an AA meeting. For *Kid Stuff*, he wrote a piece about his abusive alcoholic father. He told of how, when he was thirteen, his father put a gun in his hand and drove him around the neighborhood, calling him his bodyguard. Here, he speaks *as* his father—or, rather, an alternate version of him, a father who turned his life around (as neither of our fathers did) and whose son stands up to him and fights back (as neither of *us* did). After spending thirty years behind bars, Don embodies a man who picks up where he *didn't* leave off, becoming a real father to his adult children and grandchildren.

++++

A student recently asked me when I realized just what prison *was*. I knew exactly when. It involved the misunderstanding of a simple word. During the *Showdown* run, the superintendent walked into the gym before the family performance and told the men that after the show the families would be escorted through the side door while the men remained onstage. As soon as she left there was an outcry. They begged me to intercede so they could have time with their loved ones. I did so, fully expecting to be rebuffed. I was unprepared for her reply:

"Fine, then tell them it's a *visit*."

I bounded back into the gym bearing what I thought was incredibly good news, only to receive glum nods as the men walked away. After the show, after the tears and laughter and hugs and hollers, after everyone basked in the light the men shone on them for ninety minutes, and after the families exited through the side door, I noticed my actors heading over to the Blue Room instead of the main entrance. I asked one of the guards what was going on and he nodded indifferently:

"Strip search. Required after a visit."

A visit. *That* explained their benign response to what I'd thought was good news. That was what was exacted for months of hard work and fierce loyalty to the project and each other. That's what they got for giving brilliant and inspiring performances before a spellbound audience—stripped naked and searched in the most humiliating and invasive way. A line from "The Box" crashed through my brain:

"They've taken everything else—my freedom, my identity, and my dignity every time they look up my asshole after a visit from my momma!"

Watching the men line up, holding their coats and bags as they stared resignedly at the floor was shattering, and yes, for the first time I had some small idea of what prison is. The end of a road to nowhere in an incomprehensible world. An impossible place where you are punished for being bad *and* good. My outrage and sadness was further compounded by knowing these men willingly underwent the degradation of a strip search for hugs and kisses and congratulations. Didn't their courage and accountability demonstrate a real transformation? Shouldn't the work they do and the sacrifices they make bring redemption screaming down from the heavens, or at the very least, offer a reprieve?

Sometimes, while waiting for the van that takes me to class, I wander around the count room reading posted signs about meetings and events for the staff—the Hibernian potluck supper, company picnics, retirement parties, jubilees. It all seems so normal, so day-to-day, detaining and monitoring the lives of others just a job. There is a suggestion box mounted to the wall outside the dispatcher's office and I am always at a loss as to what anyone might suggest. Conversely, I cannot imagine there being enough room in the box for the recommendations the men in green would make, were they allowed to make them.

Every December a small, artificial Christmas tree is erected in the count room. Watching inmates assigned to the maintenance crew earnestly trim the tree with plastic ornaments and limp garland elicits an involuntary response to either laugh or cry.

> You'll never know who I am today because your focus lacks the ability to see beyond my yesteryears. You will never know what moves my heart because your sense of touch will never feel anything beyond the beat of this physical pulse. You will never be moved by the sound of my voice because your mind remains stagnated in a paralyzed state incapable of taking heed to the direction of my message…. Am I a hypocrite for using the word *never*?

Landon fires that question at the audience in a live remount of *This Is This* at HB Studio in the summer of 2022. In a sold-out run, several of the actors have the unique opportunity to reprise roles they originated in the prison production. It is our tenth production, twelve years since I first drove up to the gates of Ferrisburg for a "one-off" acting class.

I recently watched a recording of the original production of *Inside Out*. It was shot with one camera, a single omnidirectional microphone, dodgy lighting, and constant interruptions from announcements over the PA system. It is extremely moving. The discipline, camaraderie, and honesty that pour out of the men, wash over the audience, and seep through the screen are remarkable. I become so entranced by it that I forget I had a hand in making it happen, that I have learned to deal with the harsh constraints and limitations of the prison system to create theatre that lives and breathes. That I have overcome some of my deepest fears in mentoring men who would have undoubtedly bullied me as a child. That I have learned how to defuse bombs.

In one of my very first Acting Out workshops at a special high school for gifted and troubled kids, a tall angry boy in a North Face balloon jacket walked up to me as I was gathering everyone in a circle and barked:

"I ain't doing this fuckin' shit!"

After a terror-stricken second or two, I responded:

"He's not doin' this fuckin' shit. How 'bout the rest of us give it a shot."

We started a game of Ripple while North Face sulked and scowled on the periphery. Everyone laughed and clapped and snapped around the circle. He held the perimeter until he couldn't stand it anymore— until he stepped forward, joined the circle, and started doing the fuckin' shit. Those are the moments. When an angry, tough teenager surrenders. To fun, to play. Innocence. I see it in the Theatre Workshop all the time. A most paradoxical state, all things considered, but a starting point, where the possibilities are endless.

The most difficult version of the Hello exercise is a two-line exchange: "I love you." "I love you, too." The first time two inmates attempted the exercise, there was a complete breakdown. The first man choked and coughed, trembling like he was having a fit. The second man stood rigid as if before a firing squad. When they were unable to complete the dialogue, I sent in the next man, and then the next.... No one was up to the task. Reckoning that it might just be impossible under the circumstances, I told them it was an extremely advanced exercise and that I was letting them off the hook. As I started to move on, one of the men stepped forward with a look on his face I will never forget. He was going to jump, and the fucking net was going to appear! He walked to the center of the circle, looked at his brother in green, and said, "I love you." And one by one, each man follows suit.

A few months later, on a warm summer night, I climbed out of the van and headed back to the arsenal after class. A voice came bounding up the hill, over the grassy meadow that borders the road on which the men are walking.

"Love you, Rich!"

Without even thinking about the driver in the van or the CO in the tower or anybody else on the damn planet, I call back:

"Love you, too!"

++++

I am still not sure how I ended up doing what I do or how I seem to know what I know. I cannot help but think that Sister Marlene had a hand in it. I will never forget the love in her eyes when she spoke of her babies and the fervor with which she advocated for them. I always thought her greatest gift to me was permission to pursue the life I wanted, but she gave something even more important—love for those deemed unlovable.

I love the men and women with whom I work, and I do my best to protect them—odd, considering the places they have been and the things they have done. But I have no agenda other than to train my actors well and put up the best shows I can. It is the only way I can teach, keep my ego in check, stay off of "do-gooder mountain." In the end, though, I guess it *is* a kind of mission, one in which I have the privilege of creating a space in which God's kids can take a deep, cleansing breath.

ACKNOWLEDGMENTS

My sincerest thanks…

… to the scores of men with whom I've worked throughout the years for their talent, hard work, courage, and commitment to the Theatre Workshop. To my staff advisor and the administrative staff who supported our work. To the members of Acting Out for their continued dedication to creating theatre.

… to my most supportive agent, Julia Lord, who never lost faith and persevered in getting this book to print. To my editor, Chris Chappell, who strengthened and enhanced this story while respectfully retaining its heart. To everyone at Applause Books, Rowman & Littlefield, and Bloomsbury who had a hand in bringing *Acting Out* to light.

… to the many friends and colleagues who have encouraged me as a writer and actor and director through the years, and all those who made the trek upstate or downtown to attend our productions. To Francesca Ferrara, who has worked by my side for so many shows, and David Rothenberg, who continues to be my champion. To the memory of my two great mentors, Gene Frankel and Edith Speziali, without whom I would not be the man I am today.

… to the India Blake Foundation without which so much of this work would not have been possible.

… to others who put their money where their mouth was, lending financial support when needed as well as those who contributed regularly and significantly: Seward and Cecelia Johnson, Liz Feeney, Carla Barrett, Filip Kesler, Barbara Lakota, Michael Verchot, Bev Page, Deborah Schmidt, Katherine Ferrara, Guy Barudin, Anne McHugh, Michael Horowitz, and Scott and Bethanne Lewis, among others.

… to those who generously gave permission to have excerpts of their writing included in the text: Bill Blount, Joe Assadorian, Damien Walker, Joshua Gumora, Jason Morales, Kevin Ford, Haneef Washington, Ron Horton, Labre Fulcher, Natasha White, Jose Rodriguez, and KJ Steinberg.

… to HB Studio, who provided a home for the Acting Out company, and to Edith Meeks, who made that happen. To James O'Barr who started the whole ball rolling.

… to everyone who worked tirelessly on productions both inside and outside the walls, especially Azusa SheShe Dance, Naja Selby-Morton, Vanessa Tlachi, Mike Abrams, Melisa Kucevic, Nira Burstein, John Gutierrez, Rhema Boston, and Justo Hierro.

… to my mother, Pat Hoehler, a wonderful writer, who bequeathed to me her love of writing and of books. How she would treasure this one.

… to my spouse, Tom, and my son, Jonathan, the two people I admire and love the most.